Melisa Buie, PhD
Keeley Hurley
Noël Kreidler, MEd

FACEPLANT

FREE yourself from failure's funk

First published in Great Britain by Practical Inspiration Publishing, 2026

ISBN   9781788607933 (hardback)
         9781788607940 (paperback)
         9781788607957 (ebook)

EU GPSR representative: LOGOS EUROPE, 9 rue Nicolas Poussin, LA ROCHELLE 17000, France. Contact@logoseurope.eu

Want to bulk-buy copies of this book for your team and colleagues? We can customize the content and co-brand *Faceplant: FREE yourself from failure's funk* to suit your business's needs.

Please email info@practicalinspiration.com for more details.

Falling man design by Dick Skelt, Out of House

Practical Inspiration
Publishing

Contents

Foreword by Wendy Smith

In the next few months, my twins will graduate high school. Our house is buzzing. Accepted college brochures flood our mail while high school graduation details fill our email inboxes. In the rare quiet moments, I shift from tactical planning to reflection. What do I hope for my kids as they enter into the adult world? At the top of my list: Be bold. Try new things. And most of all… don't let fear of failure hold you back.

Lots of high school graduation speeches tell the seniors to fail fast and fail forward. Dr. Seuss's popular graduation book, *Oh, the Places You'll Go!*, reminds graduates that, "it's true that Bang-ups and Hang-ups can happen to you." Failure is not only an inevitable part of our lives – it's often the engine of our success. Progress depends on experimenting, failing, and then learning.

Long after high school (or college) graduation, leaders and employees continue to grapple with this issue. Just recently, I sat in a CEO's office. The company's core values of innovation and experimentation were boldly scrawled behind her desk. Yet our conversation focused on her fear of taking risks. She kept returning to the pain of a recent failure. That "icky" feeling left her stalled.

It turns out that accepting and learning from our failures is easier said than done. Which is why I'm so grateful to Melisa, Keeley, and Noël for writing *Faceplant*. They recognize the inherent tensions in failure. When we try to avoid it, we only end up reinforcing it. We get so caught up in trying to be flawless that we miss the vital lessons failure has to teach. Success doesn't come from avoiding missteps, but from learning how to walk through them well. This book doesn't glorify failure, nor does it deny its sting. Instead, it offers a grounded, compassionate approach to engaging failure when it inevitably shows up.

For many of us, failure is laced with old voices: the teacher who shamed us for being wrong, the boss who penalized every slip, the inner critic who insists that flaws make us unworthy. *Faceplant* peels back these layers and offers a radically refreshing alternative: a method that helps us learn from mistakes, move through shame, and unlock our potential.

At the heart of the book is the FREE model: *Focus, Reflect, Explore, Engage.* Think of it as a compass when you're lost in the woods. First, *Focus* brings us face to face with the facts of the failure – without excuses or spin. *Reflect* invites us to sit with the emotions and narratives surrounding the experience. *Explore* opens the door to curiosity and imagination: What patterns got us here? What alternatives exist? And *Engage* asks us to make a conscious choice about how we move forward, applying what we've learned.

Each chapter is filled with personal stories that are strikingly open and relatable. Melisa, Keeley, and Noël don't position themselves as experts on a pedestal. They show up as full humans navigating heartbreak, stumbles, and the daily vulnerability of showing up. These stories, woven together with research and real-world insights, strike a balance between empathy and action. They remind us that failure can hurt, but it can also wake us up.

What makes *Faceplant* especially powerful is how it exemplifies both/and thinking – a core idea in my own work. It refuses the false choice between "just go for it, who cares if you fail" and "avoid failure at all costs." Instead, it embraces the tension: we can care deeply about success *and* acknowledge that failure is part of the process. This mindset includes holding space for ambition and humility, risk and reflection, and enables us to learn faster, bounce back more resiliently, and stay open to growth.

The book also makes a critical intervention in how we talk about emotion. Phrases like "Fail fast!" sound good on posters, but they rarely soothe us at 3 am when we're spiraling with shame. *Faceplant* insists that we make space for that shame, grief, or anger – not to wallow in it, but to understand and process it. That emotional honesty is not a detour from success – it's the path.

And this isn't just theory. *Faceplant* includes practical tools from journaling prompts to imaginative "pre-mortems" that help readers shift their relationship with failure. These aren't one-time hacks, they're practices. And as you return to them, you build something far more lasting than fearlessness – you build resilience.

Ultimately, *Faceplant* is more than a book about failure. It's a guide to growth, grounded in curiosity, emotional courage, and compassionate reflection. Whether you're a student, a parent, a leader, or simply a human who's ever fallen flat on your face, this book is your invitation to stand back up, ask what just happened, and keep going with more wisdom, more clarity, and maybe even a little more grace.

Because failure isn't the opposite of success. It's part of the story. And with *Faceplant*, it can be one of the best chapters.

Introduction

This book is about the ultimate F – failure. In picking up this book you likely realized that the big F has impacted your life in more ways than you'd care to admit. In the title we wanted to completely embrace the funk of failure with alliteration which captures all the big fat Fs of life. All those Fs may remind us of being graded in school. Fighting for a class ranking or spot on the sports team. Fighting for a promotion or to prove our worth with all that we accomplish. Or maybe it's the F of fleeing, running away from what we don't know or are scared to try. The F might remind us of fear that freezes us or keeps us stuck. The F might cast us as a follower, afraid (or "'fraid") of standing on our own, away from the crowd, being different. Or F can vividly paint our immediate reaction to failure yelling FUUUUUDGE!

Failure can conjure up heaviness, feelings of fear, being stuck, and dread. It can feel so heavy at times that it's hard to move, so overwhelming that wanting to quit or never even start sounds like a very appealing option. Most of us would admit that one of our biggest fears is the fear of making a mistake or failing![1] Fear of failing stops 49% of Americans from accomplishing or revisiting their goals. It's not much better for Brits: 46% refuse to start something new for fear of failing. Roughly 40% of Asians let fear of failure dampen their entrepreneurial spirits. Due to the funk of failure, many of us feel emotional and can't decide and/or don't take action to move forward in life. This failure funk feels yucky and weighty – like gravity pulling us into an abyss from where there is no escape. The pull can be too great for us to feel any sense of freedom regarding failure or the excitement of those who encourage us to fail with mantras like "Fail forward" or "Fail fast, fail often." As we, the authors, started our own journey examining the failures in our lives, we experienced this funk firsthand and were often caught by failure's gravity in different aspects of our lives. We were stuck and there seemed to be no brute force means to free ourselves. Like good scientists, we decided to investigate to see if there were ways to help ease the weight that threatened to crush us. Through much trial and error, we were finally able to find a method that helped us navigate the tumultuous seas stirred up by failure.

Whether we realize it or not, failure very likely has a massive impact on how we live our lives. So many emotions can often overwhelm us when faced with a failure or even the potential of a failure. Some of these include shame, blame, denial, frustration, grief, anger, avoidance, despair, hopelessness, desperation, guilt, shock, panic, fear, among countless others. These responses are a combination of our humanness, our socialization, and even institutional rewards.[2] All these factors interplay, leading us to fear failure and avoid learning the valuable lessons that failure must teach us.

What is failure... really?

Failure is... well frankly, complicated!

Let's start with the basic definitions of failure, which include: 1) lack of success, 2) the omission of expected or requested action, and 3) the action or state of not functioning.[3] In essence, failure is anything that doesn't work in the way we want it to or think it should. Simple definitions of failure don't adequately capture the complex history and array of emotions that blindside us when dealing with failures in our lives. *Faceplant* is structured in such a way to help this complexity become clearer, so the nuances can be adequately addressed.

At this point, if you're like us, you might be asking yourself questions such as, "How do we release failure's grip so that we can examine our failures without the heaviness and feelings that weigh us down?", "Is there a different way to approach how we examine failure?", and "How can we turn failures into growth opportunities on a consistent basis?" *Faceplant* will cover all of these questions and more as we introduce a method for approaching failure in a new way. This method is called FREE: *Focus, Reflect, Explore, Engage*.

Faceplant is organized into three parts

Part 1 helps us find our footing by acknowledging the emotions we have about failure. Once we have our starting point, we dive into how we learn and what we need to do to flip the existing script on our failures.

Part 2 is all about doing the work. We'll walk through the practical steps of how to turn the impact of failure around and ease the pull of failure's gravity. As we start to view and feel failure differently, it's natural to want to share that newfound levity with others.

Part 3 is about fostering FREEdom for others by offering suggestions about how to share this work so they too can release failure's funk in their own lives.

Part 1: Finding your footing

Knowing the impact failure has had on our lives, how we'd like to relate to failure, and even how we learn is important, but knowing doesn't change anything if we don't act upon what we know. As a result, we created tools and processes that offer us the opportunity to take new actions and relate to failure from a fresh perspective. With the goal of freeing ourselves from failure's funk, here is how we structured the book. Part 1 is broken into three chapters, each one representing a piece of scaffolding that will support the work to be done in Parts 2 and 3. The first chapter covers the emotions and funk of failure. While we can be lighthearted and joke about these topics, these are very real feelings with very real implications in all our lives and deserve attention and reverence.

In the next chapter, we share the basics of how we learn and how our minds view the different aspects of failure. Spoiler alert: *Reflection* (the last thing we want to do when it comes to failure) holds the keys to unshackling us from failure's funk. Finally, we wrap up Part 1 with the process for flipping the script on failure. Self-compassion and mindset become cornerstones that allow us to leverage the power of reflection using a process called *hansei* (a Japanese word meaning self-reflection and self-improvement).

Part 2: FREE yourself

Knowing that reflection is critical to our self-improvement, learning and growth is one thing, acting on it is another. As the three of us practiced *hansei* regarding failures in our own lives, we began to see patterns emerge out of our actions. As a result, we created a method to help identify and address the patterns that may be unconsciously tripping us up. By taking one of our failures and applying FREE, our four-step method, which stands for *Focus, Reflect, Explore, Engage*, we can free ourselves from the emotional funk of failure and instead position ourselves to learn and grow. Each chapter in Part 2 provides details on how to undertake the FREE process for yourself.

With all the emotional baggage that comes with unearthing the unconscious actions we fall prey to, it can be difficult to fully address and process our failures. Using one of our favorite hacks, personification, we'll introduce the lineup of Conspirators who embody suspicious behaviors and actions that often trip us up. Once we've identified our individual response to failures, we'll spotlight those Tripping Hazards and illuminate alternative paths around them, i.e. Liberators. This is where we create a new relationship to failure – shifting what we've made it mean, becoming aware of the decisions we've made about ourselves, and freeing ourselves from the

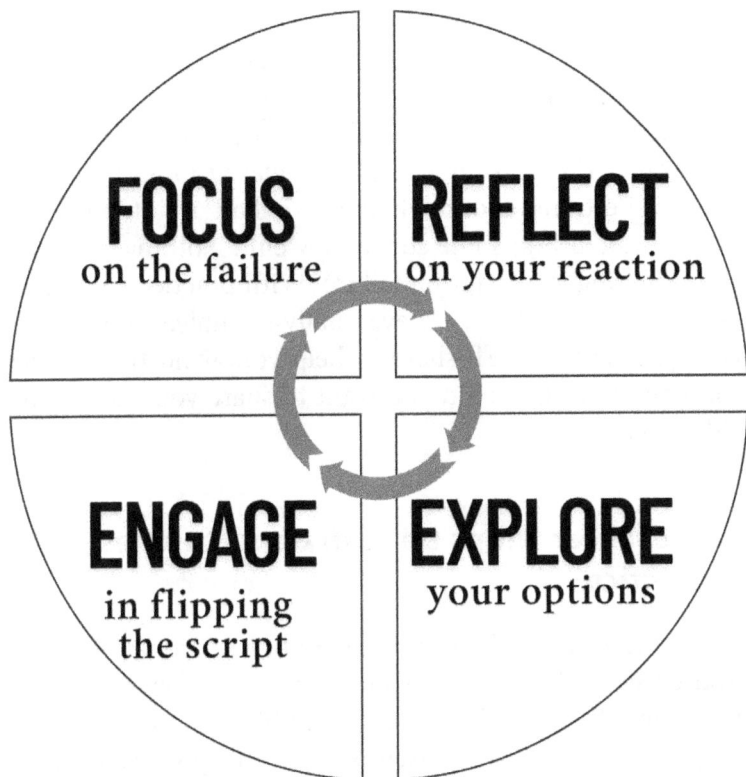

FOCUS
on the failure

REFLECT
on your reaction

ENGAGE
in flipping
the script

EXPLORE
your options

Figure 1   The FREE method

limits past failures have put on our lives. We're going to provide tools to help stop pushing down the feelings, stop avoiding past failures, and finally flip the script that has kept us trapped for far too long.

Part 3: Foster others' FREEdom

An interesting thing happened to us once we began to FREE ourselves from failure's funk: we started seeing these autopilot responses EVERYWHERE. In our friends, in our families, in our work teams, virtually no one was safe. Knowing that there was a better way to take on life, we desperately wanted to share this work with others. Our newfound enthusiasm for examining and embracing failure led us to verbally spew a bunch of new terms that sounded like jargon to our friends and family. This was often met with glazed looks and concerned questions about whether we had unintentionally been recruited into some sort of spy cult. Nothing like failing at flipping the script on failure. With practice and a few more concerned looks, we eventually stumbled onto a better approach that we'll share to help you avoid these same Tripping Hazards should you want to share your new skills with others.

Each chapter wraps up with opportunities to practice

At the end of each chapter there are two sections: "TL;DR" (Too Long; Didn't Read is a summary of the key points for that chapter) and "Where the rubber hits the road" (activities for you to complete based on the concepts discussed in that chapter). These sections serve several purposes including repetition to help solidify concepts and additional practice to drive concepts home while fine tuning your reflection skills. These are also helpful if a particular chapter isn't your vibe; skip to the end and still get the key takeaways and an opportunity to practice them regardless. Finally, these sections can be helpful after completing the book if failure's funk does a sneak attack and you need a quick refresher on the concepts.

Who we are...

At this point you might be thinking something along the lines of "Who are these crazy people, and why would they willingly put themselves (and us) through the failure ringer?"

It all started when Melisa, the brilliant experimentalist and passionate leader, Noël the compassionate career counselor and disability advocate, and Keeley, the queen of transformation, lover of all things shiny, fun, and… SQUIRREL!… came together to collaborate on a business improvement project. While COVID shut this original collaboration down abruptly, it was not the end of the story for us, merely just the beginning of our epic adventure. As time went on and the world returned to normalcy, it became more and more clear we were destined for something greater. We began brainstorming projects that were both worthwhile and sparked our diverse and often diverging interests. Taking a closer look at failure seemed to be the perfect fit for this noble cause so we seamlessly dove in – and the result is this book. Just kidding, who in their right mind would find failure easy to dive into? More like diving headfirst into a pool with no water.

Over a year after Melisa first suggested failure as a topic worth examining further, the three of us could finally begin to discuss our biggest life failures without immediately being hijacked emotionally. Once the emotional overwhelm reached manageable levels, we realized that we had identified a process that could help us start to see patterns emerging behind our failures. Patterns that had different underlying mechanisms but continued to manifest in a similar fashion in each of our lives. While the original intent was for self-improvement, we knew we were on to something that could benefit so many people who had suffered similarly through their own failures. The original work led to more research, more conversations, and more interviews with a variety of individuals. With resoundingly positive feedback, a book idea was born. Throughout the book, we've included our own stories as examples of failures. We've also included a few stories from people who have been brave enough to share their stories with us. Where we've included the true stories of others, we have used pseudonyms out of respect for the funk that may still accompany these failures.

When asked to describe how such a diverse group of women could work together on a project such as this, the image that developed was similar to how different body parts each play critical roles in a single person... Melisa representing the head: the analytical, scientific evidence and logical piece; Noël representing the heart: her empathy and deep desire to make the world a better place for people with disabilities and future generations; and Keeley representing the spirit fingers: adding spice and different ways to imagine difficult concepts (we don't really want to even guess what goes on in her mind). Together we formed a super trio of science, grace, and spunk that created a unique approach to the difficult and emotionally charged topic of failure. We aren't psychologists, but we do highly recommend seeking their guidance and support if any of this work is too heavy for you to carry on your own.

We know that the words, concepts, and emotions that failure brings up may be uncomfortable as you read this book; they certainly were for us. We won't leave you filled with useless platitudes about failure. Instead, we'll provide you with tools to experience your failures in a new light – one that's insightful, alters your perspective, and creates a new freedom around failure. All three of us have experience as leaders in business. We have coached employees through our work and pride ourselves in being lifelong learners with a commitment to personal growth and development. We are staunch advocates for the people in our lives, and as readers, you are now a part of that circle. Our goal in writing this book is to support you in your success and life fulfillment.

Are you with us on the field?

This book is not intended for those seated comfortably in the bleachers watching life unfold, but for those who are willing to play an active role in improving their lives. For those of us on the field: (In our best announcer voice) LET'S GET

READY TO RUMBLE! To get the most out of the process and exercises in this book you must do them. We know, we know, ugh, but trust us, participation is mandatory if you want to heal the wounds of failure, not just put band aids on them or cover them up with a long-sleeved shirt. Practice and reflection are the names of the game. We suggest grabbing an old school journal or notebook because there's just something about writing it down that helps release bottled emotions. It doesn't have to be pretty; this process won't feel pretty at times. If you're allergic to paper or terrified of someone finding it and *GASP* reading it, get yourself a password encrypted, multi-authenticated, face ID locked digital journal (OK, that may be overkill, but we hear you on the fear part and we'll get to that). There are a number of digital platforms that work well so feel free to grab whatever you're most comfortable with – hard copy or e-version. Go on, we'll wait. (Dramatic pause.) OK, now that you have your journal…

If you are up for it, once you are into this FREE process, find a friend/confidant/sympathetic ear to partner with on this journey. If your immediate thought was "OH HECK NO!" we get it, but really, the yucky feelings of failure that keep us stuck don't have to be the future. By bringing this out in the open you take back the power that failure's funk has stolen from you. In doing this work ourselves, we often found that we were our own worst critics and that getting an unbiased, outside opinion helped release the grip of failure. Feel free to also join our discussion group on Facebook: **The Faceplant Book**. While it might be scary to discuss failure with a group of strangers, it can also be strangely freeing to remove the fear that people close to you will judge you more harshly.

DISCLAIMER #1: This is hard work. And emotional work. There is a good chance at some point you will want to toss your hands in the air, chuck your notebook, and throw in the towel. We were there too. Do what you need to do to take a break and be gentle with yourself. Take as much time and self-care as you need, but please don't give up. Please come back when you're ready. We'll be waiting because we know you can do hard things even if you aren't completely convinced of that yourself yet.

DISCLAIMER #2: We do not all have an equal license to fail. Failure can be seen as a privilege. Being vulnerable enough to fail and talk about it doesn't take the same amount of courage for all of us. While we individually can't fully grasp the additional gravity failure exerts on others, we do want to acknowledge it. We also still believe this work is beneficial at some level regardless of our varying degrees of privilege. Let's get to work.

TL;DR

- Failure is complicated.
- Failure often induces a funk.
- We can change our relationship to failure.
- Changing this relationship is hard work.

Where the rubber hits the road

Get your journal. Seriously. It's important. Here are a few exercises to get any failure and fear of failure fresh in your mind.

- Find your failure partner or join our online community. (We love supporting people with this work.)
- Take a deep breath. You can do this.
- Dig in: Have you ever felt like a failure? When did you first feel like you failed? Write about this time and what happened. Did this lead to decisions you made about yourself or how you would live your life?
- What role does fear play in your own life? Write out all your fears. Let your imagination run wild and try creating a "fear list."[4] List everything you are afraid to

do. Analyze each failure scenario through the following filters:

1. What is the absolute worst-case thing that could happen?
2. Do you see anything you could do to prevent this worst-case thing?
3. Let's say the worst case does happen, what could you do to fix it?
4. Would there be any benefits of conquering this fear?
5. Is there a cost to you of doing nothing?
6. What would it feel like to be free of the stigma of failure?

- If fear is a particular concern and has a grip on you, use these questions to examine your fear of failure:[5]

1. Do you worry about what others think of you? Are you concerned about your ability to get what you want in the future? Are you worried about whether you are smart and/or capable? Are you afraid of disappointing people, especially those whose opinions you value?
2. Do you tend to tell people beforehand that you don't expect to succeed in order to lower their expectations of you?
3. Do you have trouble imagining what you could have done differently to succeed after you've failed at something?
4. When preparing for something important, do you begin to develop physical symptoms like headaches or stomach aches? Do you get distracted with other things while preparing for something important? Do you put off starting and tend to run out of time?

Part 1

Finding your footing

Chapter 1

The funk of failure

We have been raised on a steady diet of mixed messages regarding failure. From entrepreneurs to religious leaders to educators, we are told to fail fast and often, or fail forward with platitudes, trying to convince us that failure is a good thing. Yet at the same time, we learn very quickly from society that successes and winners are to be celebrated while failures and losers are to be avoided or even stricken from the record entirely. As we began searching for a title for this book, we knew we'd found the perfect word in funk to capture the feelings associated with failure. Failure can feel like a stomach-turning free-fall that tends to weigh us down, dragging us into an abyss. The emotions of failure are something akin to gravity – they hold us in place and make everything seem heavy. It's not just our thoughts that are heavy; our bodies *feel* it too. When the reality of a failure slaps us in the face, our stomach drops as a physical wave of distress washes over us, quickening our pulse (is it suddenly very warm in here?).

Failure gets a bad rap for good reason; the emotions that surround it usually leave us feeling miserable, stuck, and even questioning our capabilities and worth. No amount of logic or reason or "change your mindset, change your life" malarky can trick us into thinking "wow, that was a great learning experience, I should fail more often," just like knowing that a healthy diet and regular exercise doesn't make it easy for us to eat salad and exercise daily. More often than not, we ignore or hide our failures. We may even have a sort of amnesia surrounding failures in our past. We don't have a file in our memory filing cabinet titled "Mistakes I've Made."[1] This is often a coping mechanism to protect us from the negative emotions we experience in conjunction with these failures. By not having easy access to our failures, we quickly move on or pretend they didn't happen and can find ourselves repeating the same failures over and over again. Understanding the funk-filled emotions surrounding failure and the role they play can help break the cycle.

Failure: something to avoid at all costs

Grief, blame, denial, guilt, shame, frustration, and fear are typically associated with failure so it's no wonder we want to avoid it at all costs. Those entrepreneurs and educators must live in a different world because in our world avoiding failure seems like a much better idea than dealing with all that funk. Avoidance keeps us safe from the funk of failure by promising that "if you don't try, you don't fail." Avoiding failure might be another side effect of society's obsession with achievement, accomplishment, and the win-at-all-costs mentality that touts "if you don't try, you can't win." This avoidance of failure leads us to organize our lives around not failing, both consciously and subconsciously, with distractions and redirection. The fear and avoidance of failure can play a huge role in our lives. This can mean going through life just trying to survive, constantly on the lookout for the failure pit that might drag us in. Have you ever said "I'm not a math person," "I'm not a spelling person," "I'm not gifted," "I'm not coordinated," or something along these lines? Have you ever felt as if something was out of your control or impossible to learn? We may find that our failures define us with statements like "I'm not good at [fill in the blank]." Certainly, Melisa would have said this in her life. Growing up she felt uncoordinated so she avoided failing by shifting her attention and efforts to things she felt she could do – math and science. At first glance, Melisa's failure avoidance doesn't seem all that bad. However, her self-imposed limitation also limited her ability to fully interact with the world around her. By avoiding failure, she inadvertently avoided many opportunities for growth in areas like music, athletics, and languages.

Avoiding failure appears to keep us safe but it can also keep us stuck. Feeling stuck may not completely consume us in all areas of our lives but limiting even one area can prevent us from discovering our full potential. We're certainly not alone in this struggle, even highly functioning contributors in society may have different aspects of their lives where they feel stuck due to past failures or the fear of failure. By avoiding failure, we can't leverage it for the learning and growth catalyst it can be.

In most cases, however, we don't anticipate failure, which makes it hard to avoid altogether. We don't begin a new project or a new activity thinking "I'm going to fail." Instead, failure lurks under the surface, waiting for an opportunity to strike and when it does, its sneak attack launches us into a downward spiral of funk-inducing emotions.

Blame and denial are protective diversions

When failure comes knocking, blame and denial are often right there holding failure's hands ready to send us into a tailspin. "This can't be happening" and "It's all [fill in the blank's] fault" (insert into the blank: the weather, my alarm, my co-worker, etc.). These are usually some of the first thoughts that pop into our mind when failure bursts onto the scene. Blame and denial are two sides of the same coin. When in denial we will either deny the failure occurred or deny our role in the failure. When in blame we may acknowledge that something has gone wrong, but we make excuses for it, shifting the attention to bad luck, timing, near-misses, etc. We consistently blame anything or anyone else except ourselves for a failure outcome. Once we can explain the mistake, we are no longer responsible for it and can shed the emotional baggage that goes along with it. "Even when we know that we were wrong, we can sometimes go on feeling – and insisting – that we were almost right, or that we were wrong for good reasons, or simply, wishfully, that we weren't wrong after all."[2] Because so many factors beyond our control often come into play when we fail, it is much easier to point to those factors than it is to really look at what role we played in the whole situation. Owning our part can be extremely jarring, leading us to question who we really are. This can be an incredibly uncomfortable train of thought, and that discomfort can lead us to redirect our attention elsewhere or deny our part altogether. If it's not our fault or not really happening, we incorrectly convince ourselves that we are safe from the fallout.

When we shift to the other end of the blame spectrum, we direct that blame inwardly and mental self-flagellation is soon to follow.[3] Thoughts of "How could I be so stupid?" and "Why didn't I see this coming?" or "I'm such a mess" reverberate in our minds and suck us deeper into a downward spiral. Cue the knocking-the-wind-from-our-sails emotional dynamic duo of guilt and shame. Brené Brown, a shame researcher, often succinctly distinguishes the two: guilt is the thought "I did something bad" and shame is the thought "I am bad."[4] More specifically, Brown defines shame as "the intensely painful feeling or experience of believing we are flawed and therefore unworthy of acceptance and belonging." In her book *I Thought It Was Just Me (But It Isn't): Making the Journey from "What Will People Think?" to "I Am Enough"*, Brown explains one of the key factors in contributing to our shame is the feeling that we alone are the only ones who have ever done/felt this so we must hide it from everyone.[5] Both shame and guilt push us toward isolation to hide our missteps from the world and feed our insecurity. They make us believe that no one will understand, and that people will judge us harshly if they ever find out. Guilt can sometimes be a powerful motivator to change, and it can also be a heavy burden that we continue to carry, doing our best to keep it hidden from the general view. Shame, on the other hand, can seldom be harnessed productively and traps us in isolated helplessness by making us believe that if we are inherently bad, there is no hope to alter the course going forward. Shame is a common thread woven through most of our failures. We may feel like a failure in a certain area of life when something traumatic happens, but there's a big difference between failing at something we attempt and feeling like a failure. Feeling like a failure causes us to shrink inward and feel like a hollow shell of the bright, vibrant person we once were. The truth is that guilt and shame are horrible liars and gain their power by lurking in the shadows and convincing us that we are alone in our struggles. They rob us of the one sure-fire way to dampen their impact: to shine a light on them and see that most failures are shared not just by our trusted communities, but by humanity as a whole. Finding even one person to empathize with our plight can cast a lifeline that helps bring our head back above water instead of enabling those emotions to pull us further into the deep.

There are times when we encounter failures in systems that we are responsible for whether in our home or work. There may be nothing that we could have done, but we still may be quick to blame ourselves and feel responsible or feel that if we'd done or not done something this failure or mistake would not have occurred. In these instances, we have stumbled into regret.

Regrets are areas we like to hide away from others

Researchers tell us that our brains are preprogrammed for regret.[6] Many of us have regrets about things we didn't try that succeeded and things we did try that failed. Regret by its very nature has us look back at what might have been with the thought of "if only." There are several steps embedded in the process of regret. We travel back in time to the event, examine the possibilities, compare hypothetical outcomes that might have happened if we'd taken a different action, and finally, we place blame squarely on ourselves, much like we do with our failures and mistakes. We can blame and shame ourselves and end up with many regrets endlessly examining the "if only" scenarios. When regret becomes especially heavy it can evolve into grief.

Grief is another common emotional response to failure that takes the wind out of our sails. Failing at something nearly always results in a loss: a loss of material possession, a loss of opportunity, a loss of relationship, a loss of reputation, a loss of self, a loss of meaning, a loss of hope. The loss of a future version of us can be a devastating blow with long-lasting effects that are extremely difficult to process. Grief is also incredibly cunning, just when you think it has finally passed, it sneaks back in through some little memento or memory that drags you right back to where you were when you first experienced the loss. Melisa found grief and failure to be inextricably linked in the story below.

Melisa's story

One November morning in 1995, I was awoken by a phone call before 5 am. The caller was a Sheriff, who was sitting with my mother after he'd only minutes before told her that my father had been killed on his way to work earlier that morning. No! My head and heart screamed. No!

After everyone else had gone to bed that evening, I held my mother's hand as she dozed in and out of consciousness on the couch. She told me how much I looked like my father. This was a fact of which I had always been infinitely proud. I loved those blue eyes that also belonged to my grandfather. I was a Buie. BUT I thought in the moment, did it hurt her to look at me? Did I remind her of the man she had just lost? The last thing I wanted was to hurt her.

Two weeks later, I was back at my home on the west coast and working. This is where dealing with my father's death abruptly ended. Grieving was too hard. Seeing my mother's pain was too hard. I expected my father to live much longer. His death left a hole in my life, which I filled with work and very little else.

Rather than facing the grief and loss and dealing with the pain, I froze in place. Somewhere toward the end of my year of hiding from the grief, I couldn't function any longer. Because I hadn't dealt with my own grief, I couldn't be there for my family in their grief. I felt like a failure. I was lost and didn't know who I was. I knew I needed to talk to someone professionally. It was then that I entered several years of therapy. My inability to deal with my own grief and support my family through their grief is probably the biggest failure of my life.

In Melisa's story we can see a failure-grief spiral that was difficult to escape. Melisa failed to grieve, which resulted in her feeling like a failure, which resulted in more grief and so on. Grief can be a scary black hole. We fear that if we allow ourselves to feel it fully, it will drag us into the pit of despair, completely consuming any joy we have left. Its heaviness, like a cold, wet blanket, wraps us in a veil of darkness that we are afraid we may never escape.

Care and uncertainty can rapidly escalate emotions

While blame, denial, guilt, shame, and grief typically come after a failure, anxiety can paralyze us before we even get started. The mere mention of this emotion can elicit a quickening of the pulse, a rush of heat to the face, and a rock dumped straight into the pit of our stomach.

This makes sense when we look at the explanation of anxiety provided by Dr. Ramesh Perera-Delcourt.[7] He describes anxiety as a combination of us overestimating the likelihood of the worst-case scenario while simultaneously underestimating our ability to deal with that scenario should it arise. The other way we like to look at anxiety was popularized by Dr. Russ Harris who described it in terms of the following equation:[8]

$$Anxiety = Uncertainty \times Care$$

If we think of anxiety on a scale of 1 to 100, where 1 is the calmest state of Zen (think relaxing in a cool breeze on the beach, a cozy chair by a fire with a good book, or whatever your happy place full of tranquility and peace is). On the other end of the scale, 100 is the maxing out of the fear state (think can't breathe, can't move, or screaming and running like Kevin in the movie *Home Alone*).[9] When we look at situations where we already know the outcome or situations that we don't care about, we rarely (if ever) experience a high intensity level of our anxiety. On the other hand, if we care deeply about a situation or outcome *and* are simultaneously unsure what the results will be, our excitement can escalate quickly into fear. We each have unique tipping points: levels where we can manage the uncertainty and care factors or even see them as exciting (which oddly often feels the same in our bodies as fear), levels that switch to stress and anxiety, and levels that switch to a sense of fear and panic that seems insurmountable.

When Keeley started looking at where her personal tipping points were, she found a fascinating trend. She was able to tolerate and even thrive in much higher levels of uncertainty when it was a situation just involving herself than when a similar situation involved any of her kids. Because her care factor was usually maxed out (10+) when it came to her kids, she hit her anxiety and fear tipping points much quicker than she did when it was just herself. High levels of care and/ or uncertainty can escalate our emotions very quickly and launch us into the final item on our soul-crushing emotional selection platter: fear.

Fear: the grandaddy of all failure funks

Fear is a sneak-attacker that catapults us into our subconscious responses of fight, flight, freeze, or fawn. It's our brain's attempt to keep us safe by getting us out of this uncomfortable situation as quickly as possible. When it comes to failure, fear can quickly morph into pure unadulterated terror in the blink of an eye without us even being consciously aware. But boy does our body feel it… a racing heart, a quickening of our breathing, or holding our breath altogether. Fear is the evolutionary response to threats, enabling us to react without thinking to the saber-toothed tiger that suddenly springs from the bushes.

When dealing with failure, we've grouped fears into three primary categories:[10]

1. A threat to one's identity (e.g. failing this test threatens our belief in how smart we are);
2. A threat to our sense of belonging; a threat of rejection (e.g. failing to get this person to go out with us threatens our ability to be in a loving relationship); and
3. A threat to safety (both our own and people we care about) (e.g. failing to land this job threatens our income and ability to provide security for ourselves and/or our families).

Bonus points if a failure is perceived as a threat to all three. Our fear of failure can be so debilitating that even the most harmless sounding situation might feel like a threat. Fear of failure can drag us into an emotional quicksand that converts all our ordinary failures into larger-than-life demons we feel ill-equipped to battle.

Collapsing failure and fault prevents us from learning

We often collapse failure and fault and in so doing create an environment where it is not safe to highlight concerns or failures at home or in our organizations. Without a safe environment to fail, we tend to cover up or run from failure without reflecting, therefore forfeiting our ability to gain valuable insights and learn from failure. Making it safe to highlight concerns or failures at home, on teams, or in our organizations will create an environment where learning from failure is possible. With the myriads of funk-inducing emotions associated with failure, it's no wonder we often try to suppress it, forget about it, or move on as quickly as possible.

Despite how emotions may feel, they aren't inherently bad or good. The distinction between feelings, thoughts, and emotions made by author Britt Frank in the *Science of Stuck* is incredibly important in working through failure's funk.[11] According to Frank, feelings are purely physical sensations in our bodies. Thoughts are ideas, opinions, beliefs, etc., which are formed in our mind. Emotions are feelings with a story on top: "It is the stories we attach to our body sensations that create emotions."[12] We saw this firsthand in looking at the spectrum from excitement to fear and how the "story" drastically impacted our emotional state.

Who doesn't love a good story? We want to be able to explain and maybe even justify what happened. We want to put the event into a nice, well-ordered package tied with a bow. Stories allow us to do this. The problem is that while our brains are incredibly good storytellers, the tales they weave aren't necessarily true. Because we need the events of our life to make sense we contort the facts into a well-arranged story that creates a logical cause and effect relationship. This is where the narrative fallacy can muddle the story, causing us to learn the wrong lesson or amplify the fear even further.[13]

Some parents, psychologists, educators, and leaders can craft a story that allows them to see blame and shame for failure as a motivator. According to this line of thought, fearing failure and experiencing shame and blame lead to great achievement. In the minds of these parents, educators, and leaders fear of failure is not fundamentally a bad thing. In their view, there are cases where fear of failure, and shame and blame lead to a gritty stick-to-it-ness or even generate a creative spark. These flawed beliefs can be painful for us all but especially for children.[14]

Many people write about their greatest failures and how they have learned so much from these "crucible moments."[15] These anecdotes tell us that our greatest leaders are forged from the crucibles of failure. We want to believe this is true, we want to be able to get there ourselves, but the cloud of emotions surrounding failure make this path to fortification difficult to see. We hear these crucible stories when people who tell them are on the other side of their failure.

The problem occurs when we can't get past this fear of failure in our lives.[16] Getting past this fear isn't easy when the tornado of negative emotions surrounding failures feels like it left a trail of destruction in our minds and bodies. These emotions aren't here to hold us down or tear us apart, they are here to help keep us safe. They aren't just something to ignore or to try and suppress, they are signals that something is going on. We need to pay attention to these signals so we can understand the stimulus and why it's having the effect that it is. Understanding why we feel the way we do can help us learn and create the change we are looking for in ourselves and our lives.

The emotions we feel, both good and bad, can be healthy if we are aware, curious, accepting, and present. To get to a place where we can begin to understand our emotions, we must first learn to acknowledge that these emotions are completely normal to experience *and* we must practice self-compassion. Extending a level of grace to ourselves that is equal to that which we would extend to our family, friends, and loved ones will play a critical role in enabling us to continue this difficult journey to understanding. Consider the difference between being a member of a team (work or sports) where teammates or coaches/bosses constantly yell and criticize each other versus a team where members are supportive and encouraging to one another. Yelling and criticism tends to make us spiral further down into negativity while encouragement tends to make us more willing to keep trying even when something is difficult or invokes fear. For some reason, when it comes to our internal voices, we don't often allow much compassion and instead resort to yelling and criticizing ourselves. What we really should be doing is throwing a metaphorical arm around our own shoulder and re-affirming that this is hard and scary *and* that we are going to be OK. Part of this reassurance comes in the form of understanding how the brain works and how we learn, which we will talk about in the next chapter.

TL;DR

- Many of us live our lives avoiding failures.
- Blame and denial about failure are protective mechanisms. Guilt, shame, and grief are associated with protective emotional responses to a failure.
- Fear is a normal and very common (though excruciating) emotional response to failure.
- Emotions are feelings with a story on top.
- It's impossible to learn and grow to our full capability when we live in fear of failure.

Where the rubber hits the road

In your journal, find your tipping points and examine your relationship to failure.

- Using the multiplication matrix you used back in elementary school, you can quantify your excitement/anxiety/fear levels based on your varying levels of uncertainty and care. Using Table 1 as your guide, plot your levels. With a finger on your right hand pointing to the number in the top row that correlates to the uncertainty of the outcome, and a finger on your left hand pointing to a number in the left column based on how much you care about the outcome (it doesn't have to be exact, no pressure, we're just trying to get estimates), move your right hand down and your left hand across until your fingers meet. That number is the relative intensity level you are feeling about this instance. The higher the number where the fingers meet, the more freaked out you are regarding a certain situation.

The more situations you can plot, the better understanding you will get for your personal tipping points and how different factors come into play. Here are a few examples to get you started:

- Sending an email to your boss
- Writing a report
- Going for a drive
- Meeting someone new
- Trying a new food/restaurant
- Traveling to a new place
- Quitting a job
- Taking a test
- Learning something new
- Watching a scary movie

Table 1   Care x uncertainty matrix

Care		Uncertainty										
		Low				Medium			High			Oh sh!t
		0	1	2	3	4	5	6	7	8	9	10
	Low	1	1	2	3	4	5	6	7	8	9	10
		2	2	4	6	8	10	12	14	16	18	20
		3	3	6	9	12	15	18	21	24	27	30
	Medium	4	4	8	12	16	20	24	28	32	36	40
		5	5	10	15	20	25	30	35	40	45	50
		6	6	12	18	24	30	36	42	48	54	60
	High	7	7	14	21	28	35	42	49	56	63	70
		8	8	16	24	32	40	48	56	64	72	80
		9	9	18	27	36	45	54	63	72	81	90
	Oh sh!t	10	10	20	30	40	50	60	70	80	90	100

There are no right or wrong numbers here, just a sense of where you tip from "I can do this" to "Oh boy" or even "Oh hell no." Are there situations where you have a significant level of care no matter what? Your job? Your appearance? Your social standings? Keeley discovered this high-level care in an unusual place: movies. Often the butt of jokes by her kids for her emotional response to movies in general (she is a crying-at-every-Disney-movie kind of person), she started looking at why that was the case. Most producers/directors know that the key to a successful film is to get you to relate to and/or *care* about the main characters. Keeley is quick to get "sucked in" by relating directly to these characters or seeing them as symbolic of other people she cares deeply about, thus escalating her care factor (yes, she knows that movies aren't real, and no, she didn't see this connection until doing this work). Because her care factor is "artificially" high, small ticks upward in uncertainty sent her over the tipping point straight into "Oh hell no." When a movie's entire purpose is to keep you guessing what will happen next (hello scary movies), she quickly exceeds her tipping point and thus taps out with a hard-pass, thanks-but-no-thanks attitude to all things even remotely adjacent to that genre.

Chapter 2

How we learn

Ian was a recently graduated mechanical engineer. He and his college girlfriend had moved in together just after graduation. Ian was able to find his first job working with an engineering firm using his skills to build and design new products. He knew things weren't perfect at home between him and his girlfriend, but he wanted to make it work. One afternoon he arrived home a bit earlier than usual to find his girlfriend with another man in their apartment. Before he could think, he yelled at both of them and then he punched the other man knocking him to the floor. Hearing all the commotion, the neighbors called the police and the next thing he knew, Ian was behind bars. Instead of designing new products, Ian was now navigating the legal system and attending anger management classes with a big red flag on his record. In a split second, by failing to control his anger, Ian's future was altered. What had only the day before looked like a bright engineering future had now turned into forever explaining to interviewers why he had a criminal record. Housing was now an issue because many homeowners do not want to rent to people with criminal records. For a second's indiscretion, Ian would go through the rest of his life with a criminal label and much regret.

Ian's story is a perfect example of how platitudes like "failure is not important, how you overcome it is" completely miss the mark. Ian would definitely argue that his particular failure was indeed VERY important and overcoming it is a constant battle against the perpetual consequences of that one moment when he lost control. There's a lot of rhetoric out there when it comes to failure. "Fail forward," "Fail fast, fail early, fail often," "Failure is the opportunity to begin again, this time more intelligently," "Success is stumbling from failure to failure with no loss of enthusiasm," are just a few of the overly simplistic, completely unactionable sentiments we often hear. The problem is that these platitudes don't offer any means to carry them out or address the emotional baggage that comes with failure. Even though they may all be true to some extent, when we're in the throes of a current failure or haven't gotten through a failure from our past, platitudes aren't heard, and they aren't helpful. This phenomenon of not grasping the words is reminiscent of Gary Larson's Far Side cartoon where the pet owner comes home and is very angry with Ginger, the dog, for getting into the garbage.[1] He yells, "OK Ginger, I've had it! You stay out of the garbage. You understand, Ginger?" Ginger hears – blah Ginger, blah, blah, blah blah, blah, blah, blah, blah, blah, Ginger. Nothing changes for Ginger if she can't understand. Here's the bottom line: *platitudes don't create transformation – they just sound good.*

Platitudes like those above not only miss the funk that failure induces, but they also assume we are able to be rational and logical about our Faceplants and that we have the skills needed to properly address them. Acting logically and rationally is in direct opposition to one of the fundamentals of our brain's purpose: to keep us safe from perceived threats – and failure is a HUGE threat. When we look at the brain's structure and functioning surrounding threats, two parts stand out: the prefrontal cortex and the amygdala.

The prefrontal cortex is the slower, more conscious and deliberate part of the brain, and the part of the brain related to logic, planning, complex thinking, and self-control, while the amygdala is the reactive part of the brain. Psychologist Dr. Jeremy Shapiro describes these two parts of the brain as the tortoise and the hare.[2] The amygdala responds mostly unconsciously in milliseconds while the tortoise-like prefrontal cortex takes much longer. The terms "unconscious" or "subconscious" have been used interchangeably by psychologists and scientists.[3] Rather than jump into the debate in this book, we will call the phenomenon which happens outside of our consciousness our autopilot response.[4]

The amygdala is a key part of the limbic system, the oldest part of the brain that is responsible for behaviors and memories. The limbic system holds onto the memories (or natural instincts) of our ancestors to help us survive and plays a critical role in the regulation of our experiences of emotions and feelings. When our brains are stressed, as can happen with failure or potential failure, the prefrontal cortex essentially relinquishes control to our amygdala. Basically, the amygdala hijack's the logic and reason part of our brain.[5] The amygdala then gets our autonomic nervous system involved by increasing our heart rate, breathing, and blood pressure sending us into a high alert state, where we are prepared to face a threat with our fear-based autopilot reactions (fight, flight, freeze, or fawn) at the ready. As the first responder to potential threats, the amygdala was incredibly beneficial for our ancestors who had to be vigilant and alert to lions, tigers, and bears (oh my) to live another day. In our "first world" environments we rarely face life-or-death situations, but the amygdala is not particularly discerning, so it can still be activated by any fear. Fear of failure is one of the most common triggers to activate the amygdala in modern times. With scenarios like being embarrassed in front of others when a presentation doesn't go well or discovering that a mistake you made was the butt of many jokes, the amygdala responds in the same way whether the threats are to your life or to your reputation. It treats the vulnerability we feel due to failure or the possibility of failure as a threat worthy of the flight, fright, freeze, or fawn response and can even be detrimental by preventing us from taking risks like trying something new.

The amygdala's uncanny ability to bypass the processing of information and jump into protect mode without thinking is what is known as an Emotional Hijack.[6] Because the amygdala responds much faster than the thinking or reasoning part of the brain, our response to adrenaline-fueled fear can be disproportionate in most situations. Our amygdala has already taken over and determined our response before the logic and reason of our prefrontal cortex can kick in. This is what happened to Ian, which led to disastrous consequences.

The other assumption swirling around platitudes is that we already have the skills and tools needed to move forward from failure productively. This is about as realistic as assuming you are a concert pianist without ever touching a piano. The brain is an amazing tool that enables us to do truly astounding feats like learning, growing, and developing but there are a lot of things going on beyond our conscious awareness that prevent us from learning and can even stunt our growth if we aren't paying attention.

When we do pay attention to how the brain works, we find synapses that connect neurons in our brain by passing signals from one neuron to the next. New skills are developed through creation of new neural circuitry resulting in a physical change to our brain. The more you practice using the new skill the more refined and intuitive the new electrical circuit becomes. The repeated firing of these electrical signals results in the formation of myelin. The myelin acts as insulation, forming a sheath around the nerve fibers, ensuring the signal is transmitted quickly and efficiently. The more we actively practice, the thicker the myelin grows, and the thicker it grows the stronger and faster the signal fires, giving us more rapid access to the skill response.[7] Fortunately, we can strengthen our conscious responses to failure the same way. Unfortunately, failure is not something we typically like to practice.

Fearing failure is learned – and therefore can be reprogrammed

Most of us are unlikely to remember our first year of life. However, if you've witnessed an infant or toddler, you know that they are brilliant and relentless fail-ers. They fail over and over, until they figure out how to crawl, how to walk, how to talk. They know very little when they come into the world, but they learn by practicing and failing. At some point, the tables turn and the child, like all of us, learns that failing is not OK.

An obsession with achievement has led many of us to inadvertently foster an achieve-at-all-costs attitude toward failure. This attitude may have been instilled in us as children by our parents, coaches, and teachers. What happened when you brought home a bad grade? Was a failure to get an A called out in class or at home? There may have been a punishment or just a telling look but either way it became clear that a lower-than-expected grade disappointed teachers and/ or parents. As a result, we learned to dread and fear failure. Failure was suddenly bad. Some people learned to blame others or themselves as a defense mechanism against their failures. Others learned to deny failure and avoid it at all costs.

The fear of failure is likely to have been reinforced and subsequently increased as we grew into adults. We learned that winners are celebrities and that everyone loves a winner. For many people, the win-fail scale is binary: there are only winners and losers, nothing in between. There is only winning first place. Second or third place are fails. These attitudes often lead to common sayings: "Winning isn't everything, it's the only thing," or "Failure is not an option." This attitude towards failure is a part of our culture. The more we hear these messages and the more we experience them firsthand, the more fear or avoidance of failure can dominate the decisions we make each day. The more our decisions are dominated by fear, the more we repeat our autopilot fear responses and inadvertently strengthen them. No matter how many platitudes we hear from the "winners," like Alexander Pope's famous quote "To err is human," we don't believe that we are allowed to err.[8]

Understanding the structure of the brain not only helps us to challenge our beliefs about failure, but it also shows us how to create new circuits to consciously act in response to failure threats and fortify those circuits into fear-fighting powerhouses. By strengthening the connection to the prefrontal cortex, this new circuitry enables us to slow down our responses, rapidly de-escalate our autopilot reactions, and choose conscious actions instead. Failure may still be an uncomfortable setback but it's not the writing on the wall that *we* are a failure. While this is not necessarily an easy journey, failure can be a path to that new skill and a new future. If we can get past the immediate reaction of the amygdala and allow our prefrontal cortex to kick in, we can begin to discover the innumerable options for action we have at our disposal. This will take practice if our amygdala controls a lot of our life at present. Understanding how we learn allows us to better target our practice.

Understanding how we learn can help us learn

Aside from all the funk-inducing emotions surrounding failure and our brain's quest to keep us safe, several other factors come into play that impede our ability to learn from our missteps. Let's talk about how the learning curve, development zones, and modes of learning and retention can show us how to stop swimming upstream and help us leverage their natural flow to accelerate our learning.[9]

The learning curve: a perpetual roller coaster

Take a second and recall the excited feeling when you began to learn something new. Maybe it was the first day of class in a new subject at school, the first day of practicing a new sport, or the first time picking up a new board game. In those moments, the energy is palpable. We feel like we can do anything. The world is full of possibility because of this new thing we are learning. During this phase, we are learning rapidly, and we can see measurable progress with each practice.

People often think of the learning curve as a steady upward trajectory that with more practice comes more expertise. The learning curve is more like a roller coaster lurching between foolish overconfidence, a terrifying lack of understanding, and white-knuckle, holding-on-for-dear-life, stomach-dropping dips, resulting in either giving up or scratching and clawing through incremental small victories until we can finally regain our footing and begin inching forward. You may have even seen this in your own development. Have you ever stagnated or felt like you were going backwards while learning or gaining a new skill? Learning is filled with switchbacks. Some parts of learning are steeper than others, and sometimes it feels like we are not getting anywhere, just running in circles. Many of us begin to feel discouraged, frustrated, and/or resigned when we practice over and over and yet do not get better.

Hitting that pit of despair can be disorienting, painful, and even terrifying. It can force us to question our abilities, question our audacity for starting this new endeavor in the first place, and search for any way out of this horribly uncomfortable place as quickly as possible. Sometimes we take the despair as a sign that we've made a poor choice and should stop proceeding on this path. Other times we take it as a sign to dig deep and "show them" that we are good enough, smart

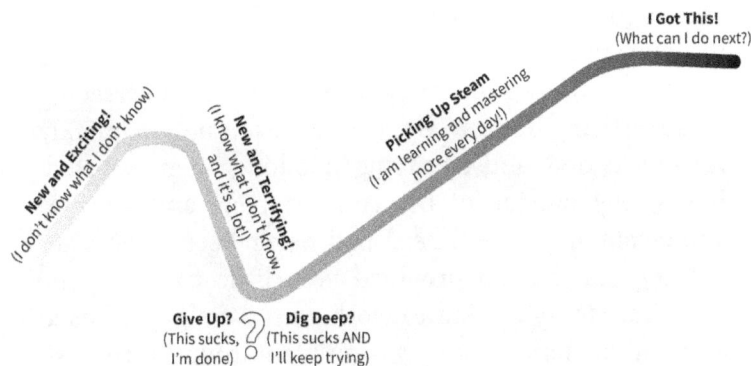

I Got This!
(What can I do next?)

New and Exciting!
(I don't know what I don't know)

New and Terrifying!
(I know what I don't know, and it's a lot!)

Picking Up Steam
(I am learning and mastering more every day!)

Give Up?
(This sucks, I'm done)

Dig Deep?
(This sucks AND I'll keep trying)

Figure 2   The learning curve

enough, capable enough to do this. Ultimately, the despair is an indicator that our expectations on the depth and difficulty of the situation were out of whack with reality, and it might be a good time to pause and consider our options. Noël had such an experience when she decided to make a career change in her early 30s.

Noël's story

After more than five years as a career counselor in the Career Services office at the University of Arizona, I was ready for a career change and a new challenge. I left my job to work in a talent acquisition role focused on recruiting contact center employees at the Intuit, Inc. location in Tucson. The Tucson site housed more than 500 call center representatives who provided customer service and sales support for QuickBooks, Quicken, and TurboTax products. Since I knew how to provide guidance to students looking for internships and jobs, and I had previously worked for IBM as a contact center representative, this new role in industry seemed like an exciting opportunity.

It quickly became apparent that I was in over my head. I transitioned from providing coaching to business and engineering students and managing one employee to being responsible for hiring hundreds of call center employees, managing a team of three, and overseeing an advertising budget. My new and exciting job quickly turned to new and terrifying not long after I started. I was way outside of my comfort zone and worried about failing all the time. I had never been a recruiter before, and the job provided very little training. The recruiting tools we had to work with were paper-based and cumbersome. There was no plan around hiring, so managers expected instant hires – like we had some sort of employee cloning operation out back. The turnover rate for contact center representatives was more than 60% in some business units.

I hadn't been in the role long enough to have solid relationships with co-workers. I was working seven days a week and did that for the first 6–7 months, often not meeting the hiring goals that managers expected. I really felt like I was failing, and I was unhappy. I seriously wondered if I had made a big mistake in leaving my previous role. I even considered resigning.

At the one-year mark, I hired a personal coach. The coaching I received helped me to see how my fear of failing was impacting my work. I decided that despite the fear of failure, I would stay. With my renewed commitment to dig into the work, I started working with leaders of other departments and making changes to the hiring process. Leaders started to invite me to their staff meetings. I had a seat at the table every week, where I had an opportunity to ask questions and make suggestions in partnership with other colleagues. Just because I decided to stay didn't mean my work was all smooth sailing. There were temporary setbacks here and there. However, between the partnerships I formed and the great work other groups were doing to address employee retention, turnover began to drop significantly.

Within two years, I went on to support the hiring process of four other call centers in the company. My career with Intuit spanned 12 years. In that time, I had many opportunities to try new roles, work in different cities, travel and develop innovative tools and processes, and I learned a ton about myself personally and professionally, especially the importance of facing failure head on.

Noël's story is an illustration of the learning curve. Learning something new usually starts with "new and exciting." It's that part of the curve where we don't know what we don't know; in Noël's case, a new job. We hit an initial peak in the first phase, and we start learning and knowing a few things, which is when the learning experience often flips and becomes "new and terrifying." Now we know what we don't know, and we don't know a lot. Noël's job became hard, and she was way out of her element. The learning curve is going downward at this point, and we are likely getting scared. We hit a bottom and question whether we should give up. This is the pivotal part of the learning curve where we have a choice to make. Do we give up because we're not sure we can do this, or do we decide that maybe we should roll up our sleeves and stick with it? It is at this low point that we are faced with a choice. Either we persevere through this difficult time, or we can give up. Sometimes giving up is the right choice. The problem arises when we don't make that choice consciously and let fear make that choice for us. If we give up, that's the end of the story. If we persevere, exploring new ways of learning, it is likely we will be able to climb out of the pit. Deciding to stay with the learning – in Noël's case staying with the job – doesn't guarantee that we won't fail or that the learning path will be smooth (as we could see if we were to zoom in on the path in Figure 3). What it does guarantee is that by sticking with it, we can learn, even if we fail.

Being aware of the valley-of-despair as we take on any new subject, project, task, or skill, doesn't make it any easier but seeing where we are on the curve in conjunction with where we are in our development zones can shed more light on the decision we are making when we do find ourselves in the valley.

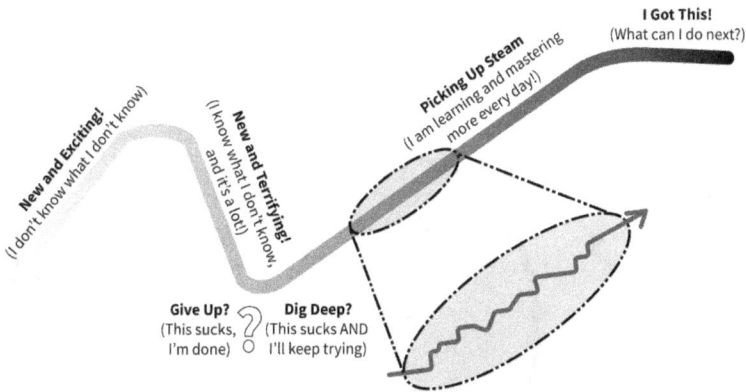

New and Exciting!
(I don't know what I don't know)

New and Terrifying!
(I know what I don't know, and it's a lot!)

Picking Up Steam
(I am learning and mastering more every day!)

I Got This!
(What can I do next?)

Give Up?
(This sucks, I'm done)

Dig Deep?
(This sucks AND I'll keep trying)

Figure 3   The learning curve magnified

Development zones: a learning tightrope

Learning often comes with discomfort. We are stretching ourselves, moving outside of what's known and safe. The trick is to keep reminding ourselves that growth and learning can only come from this discomfort. Discomfort may show itself in several different ways. When tackling a new concept in math or physics we may feel frustration over the time it takes to master the idea or solve the problem. Learning to speak a new language can be embarrassing when we try to give someone a tip (*le bout*) and offer them mud (*la boue*). We may feel anger or resentment at having to learn a new software application that isn't intuitive. All these learning scenarios are examples of moving from our comfort zone and stretching into our learning zone.

What is meant by learning zone? Using Figure 4 as a visual, imagine we are in the center of three spheres that fit inside one another like the Russian nesting dolls (Matryoshka dolls). The first sphere that closely surrounds us is our comfort zone. Visualize being surrounded in comfort. All the skills and knowledge we have gained up to this point in our life are part of that comfort zone. We are competent, knowledgeable, and effective when operating in this zone. In the comfort zone we

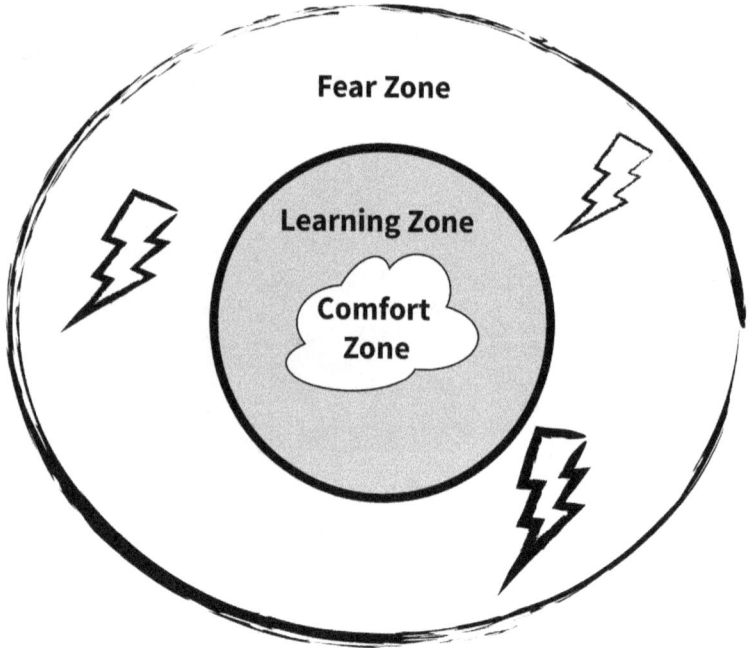

Figure 4   Development zones

are essentially doing what we know, there is no risk for us. We aren't growing as there is nothing to learn in this zone. We are safe.

To begin learning, we will need to stretch outside the zone where we are comfortable, into the next sphere, the learning zone. We need to stretch and struggle to reach this zone for learning to take place because our brain is constantly trying to pull us back to our original comfort zone. We need to stay in the learning zone long enough to get past the valley-of-despair on the learning curve and long enough for the skill to create a new neural pathway and myelination to begin. Our goal is to achieve a level of competency where we feel comfortable performing the new skill. Before we achieve that competency, however, it takes courage to push ourselves out of the comfort zone to begin learning. We are likely to experience some fear in the learning zone but with a problem-solving mindset, we can choose not to let the fear stop us. Struggle, in the learning zone, is an uncomfortable place to find ourselves. However, struggling in the right way is often where we learn. Sometimes we need to stay in that place for a while for the learning to occur.[10] Oddly enough, after enough practice and struggle, we eventually work our way back into our comfort zone anyway. This new comfort zone is enlarged and expanded after a new skill has been added to our toolbelt.

Beyond the learning zone, we enter the third sphere, which is labeled the fear zone. If we get into the fear zone, our response may be procrastination, perfectionism, shutting down, unassertiveness, or even excuses. Fear can put on the brakes and scream "NO WAY!" in our heads. Welcome back amygdala, nice to see you again. These fears can drive us to *either/or* thinking, closing doors and possibilities.[11] They can overshadow and overwhelm any rewards that might result from the struggle. If we push too far or too fast, for example, by trying to learn the Russian language at level three without fully learning levels one and two first, we may go into our fear zone and experience complete overwhelm.[12]

When fear takes hold of us it is difficult to think about anything else, but it's also a huge sign indicating that it's time to pause and evaluate which zone we are in. If we are considering quitting, we should look at where this desire is coming from. Is it coming from a fear of uncertainty and being too far outside our comfort zone, or is it an autopilot reaction in response to the fear of failure? Are we putting a higher emphasis on the possibility of a failure outcome, or are we thinking about what might be on the other side of this discomfort and what we might learn along the way? Finding a spot in the learning zone can feel like walking a tightrope precariously placed between comfort and fear. Just because our brains are wired this way doesn't mean we have to remain a victim to their impulsiveness. Instead, we can leverage various methods of learning to harness their powers for good.

Learning requires more than just study and/or practice

There are four primary paths to learning.[13] As previously mentioned, the first way is through practice. This makes perfect sense with learning languages and sports but who in their right mind wakes up every morning looking to practice failing? Not us. Practice is more than mere repetition. Practice is the struggle to overcome failures repeatedly and the willingness to experiment with a variety of approaches to find options that better position us for success. For someone to exhibit a skill masterfully, they will have had to work hard, struggle, refine their technique, and continue to practice over and over. Good public speakers often describe their process as first writing down what they want to say, then trying it out on a few people, then revising and practicing in front of a mirror or a few people again, revising and repeating until they have learned the material.

The second path to learning is through participating in rich and challenging experiences. By exposing ourselves to a variety of experiences we also expose ourselves to a larger solution space when confronted with challenges or failures. This can also be directly related to our mindset – when we choose the challenge, we see failures as part of the process to improve. At times when we stumble into unforeseen failures, we don't view them as opportunities for improvement but as impediments to our success or complete rejection of our abilities. By switching our mindset, the same failure could be merely a data point ripe for evaluation and experimentation to test if other outcomes are possible. That doesn't guarantee success, but it does provide additional avenues that make success ultimately possible rather than a tear-soaked pile of shattered dreams scattered on the floor and brushed under the rug.

The third path involves our participation in rich conversations and networks. Networks help us find jobs, locate services, find people with common interests, and so much more. When it comes to failure, however, shame often takes over making us fearful of sharing our failures with others and cutting us off from some of the very resources that can be most helpful in learning from these events. As we experiment and try things, it's important to share ideas with people and give and receive feedback. Both actions increase our solution space when faced with difficult situations. Writing this book with three authors has been an illuminating example of this process. The three of us have completely different backstories and perspectives. Yet, by coming together as a team, we have learned from each other, coached each other, and created a much more powerful understanding of failure than we ever could have done as individuals.

The fourth path to learning is through reflection. Reliving any failure can be seen as extremely painful so why would we want to relive an already awful experience? Several studies have found that we retain more information when we incorporate reflection into our study. When we read/study we retain a mere 10% of the information we are processing. If we think about how many times we have gotten to the bottom of a page in a book and have no idea what we just read, this makes a lot of sense. We can read/study all the rules of basketball, know the key terms and concepts, and even understand strategies, but without significant time spent playing the game, we likely would not make a middle school team let alone the NBA or WNBA. Through practice, we can retain 75% of the knowledge and skills needed to execute effectively, which is a substantial jump. We can retain even more through reflecting on that practice. Virtually all athletes, from high schoolers to professionals, use films of their performances to not only to reflect on how they can improve, but also to better understand how their opponents act in various circumstances.[14] The benefits according to coaches include continuous improvement, adaptation to changing scenarios, player development, and informed decision making. This allows them to be better positioned to address those actions when meeting face to face. One of the Philadelphia Eagles multi-Pro Bowl and Super Bowl champion football players credits 80% of his game to film study.[15] He's not far off. According to researchers, we retain 90% of the information/skills we have practiced when we reflect on them.[16]

Rewiring our emotions requires practice

We now know that it is possible to rewire our brains, that our amygdala can hijack us in response to perceived threats, and that there are also physical responses which correspond to a perceived threat: adrenaline rush, increased heart rate, sweaty palms, faster and shallower breaths, and blood rushing to our muscles. We can know all this and also feel like our emotions are a whole different ball of wax. The emotional reaction is a result of the external stimuli and the internal responses in our body that all happen so fast. Our brain cherry picks our memories in an attempt to predict the best response for the stimulus (threat or other). Should it be fear or anger, annoyance or sadness, excitement or anticipation? Our brains are trying to predict the future based on experiences from our past. This is really good news. It means that our emotional responses are NOT hard-coded and NOT out of our control. If we can modify the way we feel, we can modify the way we respond to a threat. While there are several ways we can rewire our emotional responses, the one most relevant to this work involves practicing the emotions that we'd most like to experience. Much like repeatedly practicing a skill, repeatedly practicing the emotions we want to experience can help our brains automatically select those emotions in the future. We reinforce emotions that we want to experience in the future (like curiosity or excitement) rather than repeating emotions of the past (like fear and dread). We can build the equivalent of "muscle memory" with our emotions, known as emotional memory, with repeated effort.[17]

Practicing emotions and scheduling reflection time are not things that typically come naturally to us. We just want to move on to the next thing and put this funk behind us. Unfortunately, by not sitting with the discomfort or digging deeper into the situation we are sentenced to perpetually running on the fear-response hamster wheel and will continue repeating our Faceplants over and over and over again. The only way off that hamster wheel is to face the discomfort by getting out of our comfort zone and looking at failure from a different vantage point: to flip the script on failure.

TL;DR

- The amygdala is the oldest part of the brain and reacts faster than other parts of the brain. It can hijack our mental processes and rational thought.
- Emotional Hijack is an amygdala hijack of our consciousness putting us into autopilot.
- Autopilot is an automatic, preprocessed response to a stimulus, particularly a threat.
- New neural circuits are formed in the brain when we learn something new. Because our brains are not fixed at birth, we can continue to learn and grow.
- Fearing failure is learned – and therefore can be reprogrammed.
- Skill retention and learning result in myelin growth. Myelin grows thickest when we study, practice, fail, and reflect.
- Learning requires four different activities: challenging experiences, practice, stimulating conversations,

and reflection. Reflection allows us to retain the most of what we've learned.

Where the rubber hits the road

In your journal, examine your relationship to learning.

- Identify experiences where you found yourself on various points of the learning curve.
- Describe a time when you experienced an Emotional Hijack and went into autopilot. What set you off? What autopilot actions did you take that you would not have if you had been able to make a conscious decision instead?
- Describe a skill or activity that you learned by using the practice-reflect-learn cycle. Can you see a way to apply this to your Faceplants?

Chapter 3

Flipping the script on failure

With so many impediments in the way of learning from our failures, it makes complete sense that we often throw our hands in the air and give up. Jumping failure's hurdles seems as unrealistic as scaling Mount Everest in ballet shoes and a tutu. In the first chapter, we talked about how we feel about failure. The emotions are daunting and real. In Chapter 2, we looked closer at our brain and how we learn. The gist of these two chapters is that 1) failure feels terrible and 2) we learn optimally by reflecting (which is not something we do when we get emotionally hijacked). Therein lies the dilemma. The good news is there are several tools that we can add to our toolbelt that can begin to outfit us properly for solving that dilemma.

Mindset is critical for learning

One of the most essential elements in how best to flip the script on failure is mindset. Our mindset dictates how we interpret failure and plays a huge role in how we respond to it.

Psychologist Carol Dweck tells us that there are two different theories about our ability to learn.[1] Those individuals with a fixed mindset believe that intelligence is fixed at birth and cannot be changed, that no amount of work can alter a future outcome. Carrying this mindset essentially makes it impossible to learn from failure. The fixed mindset sees failure as a lack of ability and gives up. Those with a growth mindset, on the other hand, believe that intelligence can be developed with dedication and effort, that "with hard work I can change." Growth mindsets see failure as a lack of progress and are motivated to work harder. "We tend to associate personal growth with determination, persistence, and hard work, but the process often starts with reflection."[2]

When looking at failure, we need to flip from a fixed mindset to a growth mindset. The growth mindset helps us to change the "." to an "...". It adds a "yet" to the end of the statement (I didn't pass the test... yet) and opens an entire new set of doors for what comes next. This is by no means an easy switch to flip. Acknowledging we are not *yet* able to do what we seek to achieve can still be a very real threat to our sense of self. That you are not *yet* an athlete capable of a marathon or not *yet* a student capable of passing an entrance exam or not *yet* an employee capable of landing their dream job can be earth shaking and hugely destabilizing. This can be especially so if a considerable portion of time and effort was invested prior to that failure. At those moments we often overestimate the distance left to traverse to achieve the goal, underestimate the distance we have already traveled, and forget the obstacles we overcame to get to where we are now.

Finding ourselves in this position with a growth mindset can be daunting but it still gives us options to eventually reach our goals instead of completely shutting down future possibilities the way a fixed mindset does. This takes us back to self-compassion.

Not surprisingly, there's a connection between mindset and self-compassion. Self-compassion does more than just help us recover from failure or mistakes. Research has shown that people who are self-compassionate are triggered to adopt a growth mindset.[3] An example of this was demonstrated when a group of students at a highly ranked university were tested on a difficult vocabulary test.

All students received feedback that they had performed poorly. One group of students were encouraged to be self-compassionate. "If you had difficulty with the test you just took, you are not alone. It's common for students to have difficulty with tests like this. If you feel bad about how you did, try not to be too hard on yourself." The other group was told "If you had difficulty with the test you just took, try not to feel bad about yourself – you must be intelligent if you got into this university." They were then allowed to study for as long as they wanted before repeating the exam. The students who were encouraged to be self-compassionate studied longer and were more likely to adopt a growth mindset.[4] Self-compassion encouraged self-improvement making the students want to work harder and do better, guided by the belief that improvement was possible. Being aware of the stark differences between the two mindsets can help us identify when we are stuck in a fixed mindset so we can flip the script to a growth mindset. Unfortunately, sometimes we can get sucked into a fixed mindset without even realizing it, as was the case when Keeley first attempted to take the Medical College Admissions Test (MCAT).

Keeley's story

Ever since I was a kid, I wanted to be a doctor. I loved science and helping people. As I grew into a deeper understanding of science and disease, my aspiration evolved into not only wanting to be an MD, but a MD/PhD so that I could be tossed to various locations throughout the world to research a shocking outbreak and be able to treat people who were suffering from a yet unknown infectious bug. I studied biology, epidemiology, diseases of animals and wildlife, chemistry, math, and physics in college to attempt to best position myself for the MCAT and future success in medical school. After graduation, I decided to take a gap year. During this time, I traveled and ended up returning to Tucson where I got a job at a laser company. Soon after returning, I decided that I would take the MCAT just to see what I was in for and how hard it was. On test day I exited the building thinking "that test was so hard I am pretty sure it killed so many brain cells I am officially dumber. Maybe I should have studied." Several months later I received the results. The exact number escapes me now, but I landed somewhere in the 50–60 percentile range of all the test takers at that time. Average. I was completely average. What I didn't realize at the time was that my scores were also sent to medical schools across the country. I received letters of interest from several medical schools. There was only one problem. The letters of interest were all from podiatry schools and I hate feet. No thank you very much. I shelved the dream of Med School, after all, I had a grown-up job developing lasers. Twenty-plus years later that dream still sits on the shelf.

This story is an example of a fixed mindset. If Keeley had embraced a growth mindset, she could have considered that being average in a population of potential doctors was not representative of being average in general. She could have looked at this as an opportunity to learn, to study, and to try again. A growth mindset partnered with self-compassion positively impacts our capacity for learning and growth and ultimately our ability to achieve in life. Both are also critical in enabling us to reflect on our Faceplants so that we may successfully free ourselves from the funk of failure.

No need to reinvent the mirror

Knowing that reflection is critical to our learning and retention is one thing, acting on it is another. Thankfully, there is already a well-established method for practicing reflection that we can leverage here. In the practice of *hansei* (a Japanese word meaning self-reflection and self-improvement) we examine our inner self – both our strengths and our weaknesses.[5]

The practice of *hansei* can help us transform knowledge into action. *Hansei* is an examination of past mistakes with a commitment to improve. There is no punishment or self-flagellation. The idea is that a regular practice of self-examination can help us to acknowledge our past mistakes. The intent isn't to beat oneself up about mistakes but to really learn and grow from them instead.

The foundations of *hansei* are twofold: 1) Recognize and contemplate one's actions and their results (looking back) and 2) Improve: both in acknowledging that no matter how positive the result, there is always room for improvement *and* commitment to using the insight of the self-reflection to make positive changes (looking forward). Looking back on our failures is difficult and often excruciating. Reflecting on our past experiences or actively practicing *hansei* is not something that comes naturally. There always seems to be something or someone pulling our attention to the present at best and off into an unpredictable future at worst. When we think about reflecting on our failures, we often ruminate on them, speculating with a lot of "what ifs" and potentially beating ourselves up with the new knowledge that hindsight has afforded us. We can also feel the physical pit in our stomach, our heart breaking, sorrow pulling us down, and weight on our shoulders all over again. This is not the purpose of *hansei*. The real purpose is to look back, reflect on past events or actions and honestly assess what went well, what could have gone better, and look forward, what (if anything) should be improved going forward.

Repetition is key in building our immunity to the funk of failure

A first step in getting comfortable with the practice of self-reflection in general is by reflecting on how far we have come on our journeys, especially highlighting the successes and obstacles we have already overcome. A key element of reflection is to continue to practice – examine all aspects of successes and failures and how they show up for us. Much like our physical and emotional sensations amplify our failure experiences, we need to leverage the physical and emotional sensations of our successes as well. Was our heart racing with excitement? Were we suddenly lighter and standing a little taller? Was there an extra pep in our step? Were we beaming with pride? Channeling the full physicality of our positive experiences can be an important component in building our failure immune system and using our bodies to help flip the script. Any evidence you can collect that illustrates you can do hard things, can overcome obstacles, can bounce back, and can succeed helps stoke the warm, illuminating fire that fights off the cold, dark, heaviness of failure. When looking for evidence of success, situations do not have to be exactly the same. We don't need to look for past examples of passing an entrance exam if we are struggling with failing an entrance exam. The examples just need to demonstrate ability: ability to pass a class, a quiz, or a homework assignment; ability to land a job, get to the final round of interviews, get an interview in the first place; ability to try a new restaurant, a new dish, a different type of cheese. All of these may seem like insignificant results, but our lives are full of these successes that we too quickly brush aside in pursuit of the next great thing. These seemingly small steps turn into a marathon of progress over time. We need all parts of ourselves – the failures and the successes – to be whole. An orchestra doesn't make its amazing sound with only the first chair performers or the solo violinist.

Seeing a more complete picture that includes our success and failures, adopting a growth mindset, and practicing *hansei* are the solid foundations on which we find our footing and brace for facing our failures head on. Using the FREE model, *Focus, Reflect, Explore,* and *Engage,* with our failures, we will build on that foundation and construct an entirely new relationship with failure – a relationship where we can learn and grow even when it does still occasionally make us nauseous.

TL;DR

- Our mindset is critical for learning from failure.
- Rewiring our emotions takes practice.
- Learning from reflection requires more than just looking back. Learning requires interrupting an Emotional Hijack and then taking the time to practice *hansei.* The FREE (*Focus, Reflect, Explore, Engage*) Model, based on the practice of *hansei,* will allow us to learn from our failures.
- Repetition is a key ingredient in building our failure immune system.

Where the rubber hits the road

In your journal, examine your relationship to your emotions.

- Reflect on different emotional memories in your life:
    1. Think of times when you have felt deep fear and dread. What types of threats were you afraid of?
    2. Think of times when you felt happy and joyful. What was going on around you?
    3. Think of a time when you were curious or felt awe. Write about the circumstances surrounding this situation.

4. When you think of failures in different areas of your life, what emotions are evoked? Where do you feel fear?

- In your journal, now reflect on your mindset.

1. Why do you think you have been successful?

2. What decisions have you made about your failures?

3. Do you assign success to your intelligence or your work ethic?

Part 2

FREE yourself

Chapter 4

Focus on the failure

Valuable insights can be gained through the major events in our lives, especially our failures. Using self-reflection as a tool, we can illuminate events (successes and failures) of the past, examining them closely to see what we can learn, synthesizing our findings into lessons for our future selves. By asking ourselves questions, self-reflection allows us to glean insights. If we don't reflect on our experiences, these lessons pass us by without any learning or growth. But we can't reflect on what we can't see, so our first step must be to focus on our past failures.

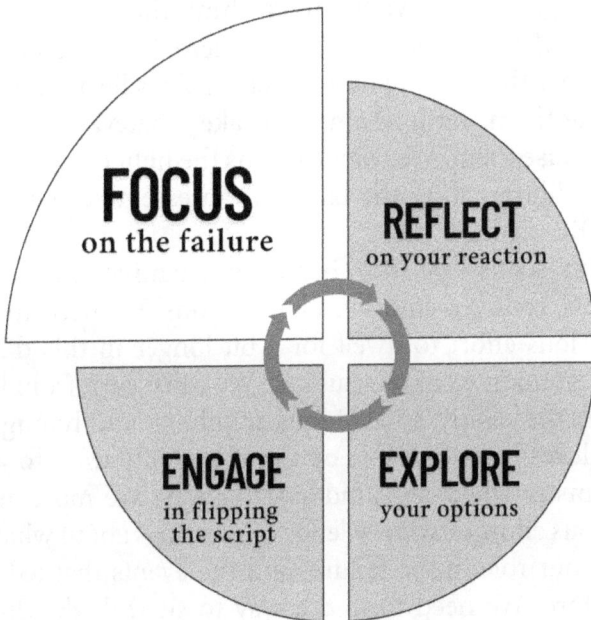

Figure 5   Focus on the failure

There are several ways to practice the focus piece of self-reflection. Keeping secrets, maintaining silence, and ignoring our failures block us from authentic openness. One of the requirements for us to grow is to be vulnerable with our own fallibility. To do that, we must expose, at least to ourselves, our failures. There are two well-researched and thoroughly developed methods of self-reflection that help us pursue focus and glean clarity: writing and sharing. These techniques may be used separately or in conjunction with one another.

We can't fix what we can't see

At times, we may think that being stuck with the result of failures from our past isn't so bad. It may not be impacting our day-to-day life, at least not in a way that we notice. We may have missed whatever lesson there was in the past but why go back now? We often think that whatever happened in the past should just stay there: "Let sleeping dogs lie." Rather than letting those sleeping dogs lie, we are going to shake them, rattle them, and take whatever actions we can to rouse them. We want to focus the light on our failures because illuminating the failure is an essential first part of the FREE method.

With focus, we can begin to examine our deepest thoughts, feelings, emotions, and actions. We need to make a conscious effort to dwell for a bit longer in this discomfort, the funkiness of our failures. We can't learn from things we can't see clearly, so avoiding, numbing, and hiding from our failures is not a viable option if we truly want to get off the hamster wheel and find a better way. We must make a conscious effort to acknowledge our feelings about what happened, our role in the failure, and the events that led up to the failure. We need to find a way to sit with the discomfort because growth happens outside of our comfort zone.

Figure 6 Illuminate the failure

We can easily go into autopilot when dealing with a failure, which allows only rigid, narrow, and non-novel thinking. We can temporarily tune out the painful feelings in an attempt to protect ourselves from the consequences of a failure, but the cost is tremendous and can also get us stuck in a pattern of reactivity to the world. In autopilot, we may delve into work, hobbies, or activities to avoid conscious activity. Recall Melisa's story about failing to grieve for her father by fully immersing herself in her job. All of us need a little reprieve sometimes by going through the motions in life. However, in Melisa's case, consistently avoiding being fully present and conscious in her life led to additional problems. When we are in autopilot mode, we are not in control and there is no opportunity for learning. Attempting to avoid unwanted feelings and thoughts by reverting to low-level thinking (autopilot), compulsive behaviors, or some other distraction strategy may provide a temporary diversion. We have millions of distractions at our fingertips, which, if we allow, can sidetrack us from reality.

We don't claim that the *Focus* phase will be comfortable, not by any stretch of the imagination. Self-reflection doesn't come naturally or easily to many of us – people tend to love it or hate it, even fear it. In general, we don't want to examine our lives too closely (especially not focusing on our failures) or spend time with our thoughts and feelings. Remember, reflection has been shown in some cases to be more effective than practice alone for learning and growth. However, studies have found that many people would rather get an electric shock than spend time in reflection.[1] Sadly, we humans would rather charge ahead, faster and faster, doubling down on practice, than pause and think things through. One study found participants were four times more likely to choose practice over reflection.[2] However, those participants who chose reflection outperformed those who practiced. Another study found that university students who practiced reflection were more likely to receive job offers, and they also received 10% higher starting salaries.[3] One study found that in team settings, the students who practiced reflection were more likely to be seen as leaders by their teammates and could more effectively articulate the story of their learning in school to interviewers. All this research highlights how valuable focused reflection is for our healing, learning, and growth journey. By avoiding the temptation to escape reality and instead face these difficult situations from our pasts, we can help ourselves to learn and grow.

Focus requires us to sort the "what's so" from the other stuff

In the 1950s there was a television detective, Sergent Joe Friday, who became famous for the line: "Just the facts, ma'am."[4] Similarly, by focusing on the failure, we want to get to the "Just the facts" level in our stories. Emotions are rampant in some failures, especially when the failure was traumatic. In these instances, meaning can get added, and the facts or "what's so" can be displaced. Funk-filled emotions are very natural responses to failure; however, these emotions don't help us learn. Our emotions have stories wrapped up in them. It might be helpful, or even necessary, to write specifically about the emotions surrounding some failures.

Focusing on the failure isn't the time for self-flagellation or blasting another person. The focus on the failure step challenges us to keep the attention on what happened. It might be helpful to think of this step as recording what a video camera would have captured, and yes, it may be difficult not to let our personal sensitivities leak into the reflection here. As opposed to assigning blame, when appraising the situation throughout this chapter keep the focus on what we know to be true. Focus on the facts surrounding the failure, while keeping the facts separate and distinct from any stories or emotions about the failure. Focus on getting to "what's so" rather than "who's to blame." Blaming ourselves or others prevents us from learning from our failures. This is a perfect opportunity to practice a growth mindset to keep the focus away from blame.

The experiences that provide some of the most valuable lessons are often the most challenging to attempt. Cringeworthy moments can be painful memories that continue to elicit many upsetting emotions. Focusing on failures isn't about ruminating on our past. Rumination makes us prisoners of our own thoughts. Obsessive thoughts become larger and larger the more we dwell on them. Trying something like meta-cognition, a technique where we step outside ourselves and reflect on the failure from the third person perspective, can create some distance between ourselves and the event and prevent our emotions from getting in the way of our objectivity. For example, instead of "My failure was…", we shift to "Noël's failure was…". This subtle change may help to reframe the failure and allow us to reduce our negative emotions.

Our growth may require us to dismantle our old "infallible self-image"

Paul Tournier wrote: "Nothing makes us as lonely as our secrets."[5] Many of us keep our past failures very close to our vests. We don't share them openly. In most cases our failures are deep, dark secrets that can be painful and uncomfortable to recall. By not seeing the light, secrets continue to have a deleterious effect on our minds, hearts, and bodies.

Mental and physical processing power is required to keep a secret. We must consciously hold back and restrain ourselves from sharing with others. The process of actively holding back information prevents us from organizing the information and creating an integrated picture. When our minds are constantly trying to process information, we tend to obsess (overthink) to try and make sense of it. Holding back emotionally puts a toll on our physical health, changing our biology, and causing long-term health effects. Disclosure releases the hold that secrets have on us and allows us to gain perspective and understanding. Putting the secret into language can provide a new perspective of what happened and allow us to begin to put it behind us.

Secrets perpetuate silence – the absence of voice. They are hidden parts of ourselves or actions we have taken that we deem unacceptable to share with others. Our inner voice often dictates the parts of ourselves that are worthy of sharing and the parts of us that must remain hidden for us to be accepted and connect with others. Ironically, the very fact that we have a secret prevents us from truly, authentically connecting with the people in our lives. Brené Brown wrote: "Owning our story and loving ourselves through that process is the bravest thing that we will ever do."[6] We can't be silent and secret and brave at the same time. The discomfort of facing our failures, whether they are spoken aloud or written, is essential to the healing, learning, and eventually growing process. Connectedness is one of the qualities we value most as humans. Our silence and these secrets are the walls that keep us from true connection. When we don't shine the light on our failures, we build up a fortress around ourselves that impedes our ability to authentically connect with others. The walls we put up to protect ourselves from this pain creates a barrier to the authentic connections we are so scared to lose. Keeley experienced this firsthand in a seemingly innocuous experience with her best friends.

Keeley's story

On a recent girls' trip, I shared a hotel room with my two best friends since high school, Erika and Jamie. For the first two nights, I shared a bed with Erika but struggled to sleep, in spite of Erika being a dear friend. By the third night, I was a complete wreck. I desperately wanted to switch beds or have Jaime switch with me so I could have a bed to myself. A mental tug-of-war ensued over what to do. I needed sleep, but I was concerned about offending my friends or seeming selfish.

That evening as we got ready for a nice dinner, I gingerly brought up the sleeping arrangements, dancing around the subject at first, instead of just asking the question. They looked at me with a mixture of deep concern and confusion until I finally blurted out the question. "Would you both be OK changing the sleeping arrangements?" Erika and Jamie burst into laughter and tried to regain composure. "That's it? We thought you wanted to go home or were getting a divorce or had cancer or something!" They gasped for air between fits of laughter. I joined in too.

In this example, Keeley realized her mind had blown their possible reactions WAY out of proportion and created a barrier that simply didn't exist. So, how do we shine the light on our failures, secret or public, and see them for what they really are, not the cloud of negativity that shrouds them? While there may be several different ways to accomplish this, there are two well-researched and heavily documented methods. The first method is by writing about our failures. By writing about our failures in the form of stories, we can begin to create a complete picture of what happened. The second method for getting clarity about our failures is by sharing our stories with a trusted confident. Sharing our stories brings additional insight to the true impact of failure allowing us to better understand the hold of failure's gravity and set it free. These methods, used either individually or together, help us to see through the dark cloud of failure's funk.

Writing opens doors to new ways of looking at your world

Isaac Asimov once said: "Writing, to me, is simply thinking through my fingers."[7] Writing allows us to capture what our brains are thinking, our hearts are feeling, and our bodies are experiencing. While thoughts may be jumbled in our heads, writing allows us to organize and process those thoughts, especially complex or traumatic events. We can examine our expectations, our process, and the outcome with a pen and paper. The messiness of the process can become a clear and concise story with writing. It's not easy, as a matter of fact, it's downright difficult. Yet, the greater the complexity of the thoughts we are struggling with, the greater the benefit from writing.

One way to untangle the complexity is through expressive writing. The practice of expressive writing was developed and studied extensively by James Pennebaker.[8] Pennebaker found that expressive writing was an effective way to work though the barrage of emotions, feelings, and thoughts that engulf us when we fail. Expressive writing is a practice of writing about an experience for 20 to 30 minutes a day. The power of writing to aid in creating a perspective on an experienced trauma has been studied for many years. The process is simple (OK, it sounds simple):

Step 1: Open a notebook or blank page on the computer.
Step 2: Set a timer for 20 or 30 minutes.
Step 3: Write, don't filter, don't worry about punctuation, grammar, capitalization. Just write until the timer goes off.

The conditions may need to be right for us to get the maximum benefit. Find a place and time to focus on the failure event – capture any feelings and thoughts about the incident. We may experience sadness or upset as we write. Despite this, keep writing: we should let ourselves get absorbed in the process and get as much down on paper as we can while recalling the event. To keep the process moving forward, we use self-reflection to examine our deepest thoughts and feelings. Asking ourselves questions can provide prompts for further exploration.[9]

Don't write for anyone else. We want to write only for ourselves with no intention to share our writing. The way we write, what we say, and how we express ourselves will be tailored to who we are writing for. If we are writing only for ourselves, we can be completely honest without fear of any criticism or repercussions.

The expressive writing practice is about writing to help us work through a situation in our life. If we get stuck when faced with a blank paper, here's some other things to try:

- Let each entry begin with a headline. The headline should capture the major event/outcome or maybe the feelings/thoughts that are on your mind.

- Ask questions to help bring in a more grounded perspective. As authors, we looked at stories we wrote and we asked a series of questions to get to the facts. One question that was helpful to us was to repeatedly ask "why?" and with each "why?" try to achieve a deeper level of understanding.[10]
- Recall and write about the emotions experienced and what exactly triggered them. Write about the thoughts, feelings, and concerns about this experience.[11]
- Experiment with writing and typing. Although writing longhand with pen and paper may not seem like a very efficient process, it does allow us to slow down and reflect so learning can happen. Brain scans show that using a pen and paper activates more areas of the brain than typing. Recent research indicates that writing longhand with pen and paper helps cement pathways in the brain and facilitates learning. Other research shows that we can learn better from notes that we've written by hand. Play with writing in cursive, or drawing scenes to represent what happened visually, or try typing. See what works.

The process of writing helps us in at least four ways by:[12]

1. **Clearing the mind**. The expressive writing process allows us to organize and integrate the whole perspective on the event/outcome. Working memory is freed up allowing us to see our failures more clearly, facilitating cognitive growth as we move from a collection of thoughts, feelings, and actions to developing a cohesive story about the failure. Melisa begins each day with a 10-minute writing exercise to clear her head. There are times when writing feels more like a laundry list of to-dos but once on paper these items no longer need to clutter up her working brain.

2. **Resolving "troublesome experiences" that get in the way of important tasks**. It's important that we experience and fully feel the failure and the losses associated with the failure. We may even need to wallow a bit with the disappointment and negative emotions. However, to avoid getting stuck in this place, we need to limit the time we spend wallowing. In summary, acknowledge what happened, and thoughts and feelings around what happened, and don't get stuck.

3. **Acquiring and remembering new information**. We can examine what the outcome means to us, including what we think it means or what we think that others think it means.

4. **Fostering problem solving**. Mindful writing and thinking are a part of active problem solving, looking at the world from many different perspectives. Being mindful is being still, attentive, and centered.

Sharing our stories gives us the opportunity to heal ourselves

Another way to quell that failure funk is by sharing our story with someone we trust. Writing isn't for everyone. Some of us may prefer talking – and choose to share our story with someone else. If you prefer talking to work through what you are feeling or thinking, you might consider sharing with a friend, a coach, or a therapist.[13] It's natural to want to talk to others about what's happening in our lives. When we involve others in our personal stories, we can create a deeper connection. Time and time again, as we (the authors) worked at refining our FREE process, we gained an incredible amount of insight, understanding, and self-compassion by sharing our stories with each other. By being an outsider who wasn't directly slapped in the face by the failure, we could provide a perspective from a much less emotionally charged vantage point and even see patterns starting to emerge that were previously completely hidden from view.

Before selecting and approaching someone to talk with about our failures and what we are seeing for ourselves in this reflective process, we need to ensure we are clear about exactly what we want from the conversation. For this *Focus* step to be the most effective, we need to know the type of conversation we want to have and be in a place of wanting to release the story's hold on us. A good question to think about before engaging is "Do you want to be helped, hugged, or heard?"[14]

When we want to have an emotional conversation with someone, it's important to set the stage and be clear about our needs for the conversation. Effective communication requires that both the speaker and the listener are aligned on the type of conversation. Do we want a sounding board or help fixing something? People who love and care for us may automatically want to jump in and help. It's important to know ahead of time what we want from the conversation. Do we want the person we share with to ask clarifying questions? It's important we let our trusted person know what we'd like to get before we begin the conversation. What if our story triggers a memory for the confidant we share it with? Do we want them to share as well? Are we OK with back and forth, or do we just need some time to be heard? It's sometimes difficult to grasp the whole situation in one conversation. Having a clear idea of what we want from the conversation before engaging with another person will help minimize miscommunication.[15] Surprisingly, no matter how close they are to us, people don't naturally understand what we want from a conversation based on the signals we are sending. As a result, it is important that we share what we want from the discussion and continue to experiment with different types of conversations.

Here's an example of what we mean. In the process of looking at failures in her life, Noël decided to write about an experience where the failure brought up a lot of emotions. She felt ashamed about what happened, and she had never shared how she felt with anyone. Once she had finished writing the story, she consciously chose to share it with Melisa and Keeley and asked them to listen – not ask questions and not feel bad for her. Through writing she was beginning to see the impact of the failure on her life for the first time, and she wanted to share it without interruption to see if any new insights emerged. By establishing what she wanted from Melisa and Keeley in the conversation up front and letting them know, she felt listened to and experienced the gravity the failure's impact had on her life.

Noël's story

There is a perimeter bike race in Tucson, Arizona every year in November called El Tour de Tucson. It's very prestigious, and people come from all over the world to participate in the race. I always secretly wanted to ride in it, but never told anyone, until one day when my boss and I were having a conversation six months before the race. I shared my secret dream with him. He then said: "If you want to do this, I will ride with you." People who know me know that I love a challenge, especially a physical challenge that seems impossible.

Why did this seem impossible? Because of my disability, I would need to ride a 60-lb 3-wheel bike 26 miles over lots of different terrain. At the time I agreed to take this on, I could only ride about two miles before I was exhausted. I started training, and my then husband agreed that he would ride with my boss and me. By the time race day came, the longest distance I had ever ridden was 13 miles. I needed to double my distance on race day to complete the race. That seemed impossible, but I was going for it anyway, and I had great support.

The race started at 12:30 pm and by 6 pm just about everyone had passed me by on the route. My body was really hurting – my bad knee, my partially dislocated hip and my right ankle – and I still had quite a way to go over lots of hills on narrow roads. On top of that it was getting dark. My boss and my ex made it OK for me to stop if I needed to, but I kept going. My boss knew I needed some motivation to continue and maybe finish the race, so he called a close friend of mine from work and asked him to come with his truck and drive behind me with his lights on. That way we could see in front of us on the dark roads and be protected from cars. At about 9 pm, I made it to the finish line. I was the very last racer. I couldn't believe it! I made it! I cried my eyes out as I got in the car to go home. Without the support of so many people, I wouldn't have been able to do this.

But here's the kicker – there is a HUGE failure here. Yes, I completed the race and did the most amazing physical thing I have ever done in my life, but I hurt my ankle in the process. And I hurt it so badly that I sustained a permanent injury, and I've never been able to ride my bike much since then without having terrible pain. Even without riding, I often have ankle pain. I failed to take care of myself – my need to prove to everyone that I could finish the race became more important than taking care of my body.

Neither writing nor talking about our failures are a magical cure-all. Noël can't all of a sudden ride her bike because she wrote and shared her story. However, by writing and talking about her failure to take care of her body, and the loss it caused, she now has the possibility of making different choices when faced with similar circumstances in the future. We can use writing and talking about our failures as a kind of preventative maintenance to potentially avert unhealthy patterns in our response to failure. There are strengths and weaknesses to both approaches. Our writing doesn't judge us, nor does it give us valuable feedback from another's perspective. We don't want to let our writing substitute for a confidant or turn our confidant into a dumping ground. Writing can help us sort our thoughts, and another person's perspective may help ground us and provide a valuable reality check.[16] It doesn't have to be an *either/or* situation – often the best solution is some combination of the two.

Knowing that we retain the most knowledge by reflecting on subjects and experiences doesn't mean we are eager to start the learning process. With all the negative connotations and emotions clouding the memory and events, it's incredibly difficult to sift through the fog and really focus on the details of our stumbles and Faceplants. This process can be difficult at times and downright devastating at others. On more occasions than we can count, one (or all) of us were reduced to tears as the heaviness of these situations pulled us downward. Please be gentle with yourself as you do this challenging work; take breaks and seek help if you need it.

TL;DR

- We can't fix what we can't see. Without investing time and energy into examining our failures through reflection, we can't learn from them.
- Focus requires us to sort the "what's so" from the stories we tell ourselves.
- Our growth will require us to dismantle our old "infallible self-image."
- Our failures may not be known to those around us and having a secret creates a barrier preventing true communication.
- Authentic connection requires that we open ourselves up and be vulnerable.
- Writing opens doors to new ways of looking at your world. Expressive writing has been shown to be an effective tool for working through complex, multi-sensory information.

- Sharing our stories gives us the opportunity to process our failures. Before we have a conversation with people in our lives, it's important to ensure alignment. Let them know what you need out of the conversation.

Where the rubber hits the road

In your journal, create a master failure list.

- Highlight a few momentous failures that had a huge impact on your life or attitude. Do you recall what you were feeling?
- Highlight a few failures that are still raw for you. You'll know which ones they are because when you see them on the list, you still have a pit in your stomach. Try your best to examine your feelings.
- In the Toolbox at the end of the book, Tool 1 is an example of a Failure Resume written by Noël. If inspired after reading hers, try writing one of your own.
- There is no one correct way to participate in or practice expressive writing. Just because something works for the authors, or for others, doesn't mean that it will work for you. Try different things until you find what works for you. (By the way, this is the type of experimentation that we will talk about later in the book.) Keep notes, monitor and track behaviors, feelings, thoughts, and activities. Check in with yourself to see if there is an effect on your sleep, your relationships, your weight or blood pressure, or mood. Adopt and adapt tools and techniques that work best for you.[17]
- Step outside yourself. Try viewing and writing about select failures from outside yourself – as if viewing them from a video camera. What, if any, difference do you notice? Was it easier to write? What feelings arose in both cases?

Chapter 5

Reflect on your reaction

If you've made it this far and are still with us, high five to your hard work! We've still got some difficult work ahead of us, but this is where things start to get interesting, so buckle up. We've examined how failure can trigger intense fear and send us into autopilot responses, and in the last chapter we initiated the reflection process by recalling and focusing on the failures, feelings, and thoughts that we've experienced. In this chapter, we are going to continue that reflection and take a closer look at our autopilot responses. You might be thinking, if they are autopilot responses, how are we supposed to see them? Much like a computer executing programs in the background on startup, our autopilot responses whir along without us having to think about them. In most cases this is a good thing and keeps us from being overloaded with decisions every second of every waking moment of every day and night. The problem arises when the *reactions* we have in autopilot are based in fear, clouded in negative emotions, and are in stark contrast to the *actions* we would take if we were able to make a conscious, rational decision. These pre-programmed responses are running behind the scenes, but that doesn't mean we can't find them if we know where to look. By shining a light on them as we did on our failures, they not only become visible, but our reflection on them can also reveal patterns and even predict reactions in the future.

As a way of painting a more vivid (and less emotionally burdensome) picture, we have personified these autopilot reactions and dubbed them as our Conspirators. They are conspiring behind the scenes, shrouded by our emotions,

FOCUS
on the failure

REFLECT
on your reaction

ENGAGE
in flipping
the script

EXPLORE
your options

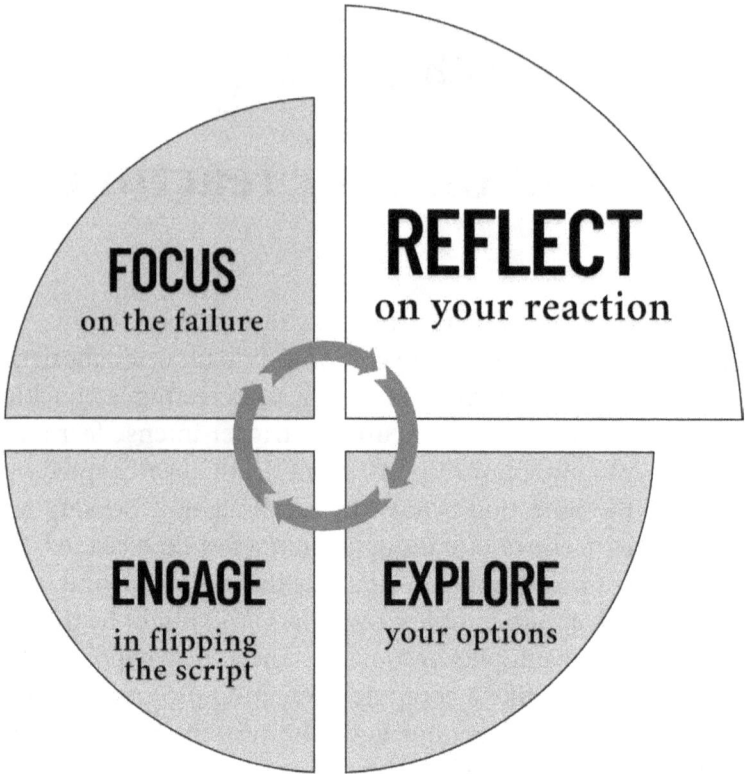

Figure 7   Reflect on your reaction

egging us on to react in repeated, predictable ways – attempting to keep us safe but really keeping us trapped in a fear loop instead. Once entwined in the autopilot fear loop, the only options that are available to us are more fear responses.

An Emotional Hijack brings out our Conspirators

When we are faced with a threat like failure and become emotionally hijacked, we typically respond automatically in one of four ways: fight, flight, freeze, or fawn. Our Conspirators, these automatic responses, act in ways that help us to either avoid the

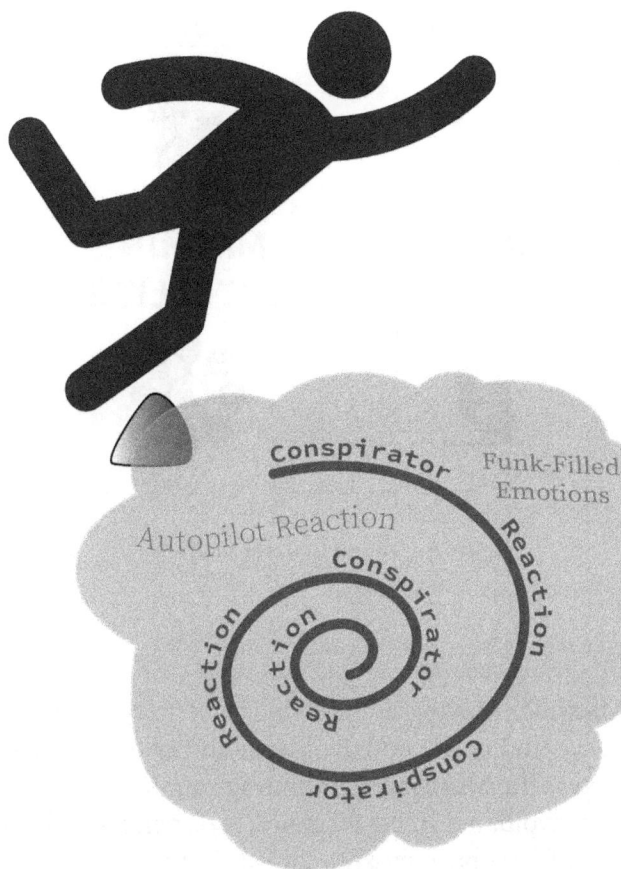

Figure 8   The conspirator spiral

perceived danger altogether or gain some perceived semblance of control over the danger. The avoidance or control that our Conspirators exert is either passive or active. To illustrate these responses, in Figure 9 we placed them into a four-quadrant grid, like a windowpane, of fear responses. The window grid illustrates what our Conspirators are doing (avoiding or controlling) and how they are doing it (actively or passively). By arranging them on this grid, we see the characteristic responses pop out. Starting in the upper right corner we see a pairing of active and control in the form of fight, personified

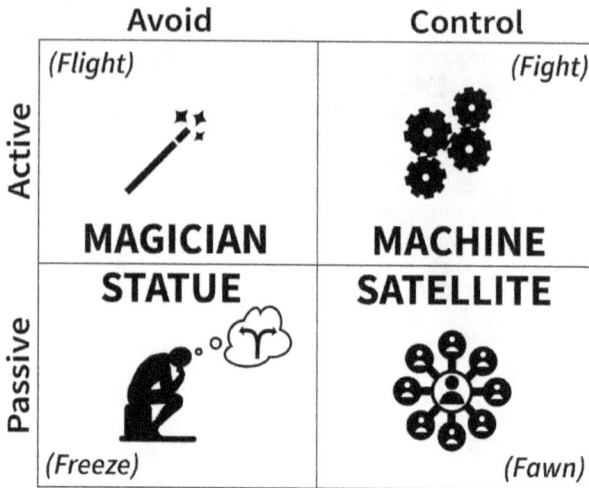

Figure 9   The conspirator matrix

as the Machine. Moving counterclockwise to the upper left quadrant we find active and avoidance in the form of flight, personified as the Magician. Continuing counterclockwise we find passive avoidance in the form of freeze, personified as the Statue. Finally, we have passive control in the form of fawn, personified as the Satellite. Let's take a closer look at these Conspirators and find out how we can spot them.

These conspiratorial responses are not necessarily good or bad, right or wrong. They can be both. The important thing to remember here is that any reaction when we are operating in autopilot mode during an Emotional Hijack is a situation where we aren't consciously making the decisions about our actions. Because our Conspirators are autopilot responses to an Emotional Hijack, we are NOT allowing our prefrontal cortex to participate and really rationalize the situation. When we've been emotionally hijacked, our automatic responses are limited to these four options and sadly there is no room for learning or growth when we operate in autopilot. As we go through each of these Conspirators in more detail, think about your own response to the failures you focused on in the prior chapter.

The Machine Conspirator must continue at all costs

Let's start in the upper right corner of Figure 9 with an active controlling response to a failure or threat of a failure: the fight response persona named the Machine. When we think of an individual with a very active fight response, we may naturally think of the person in our lives who is hot-headed and is prepared to either physically or verbally dominate to get their point across. However, the Machine's Emotional Hijack can take other forms as well, such as someone who keeps fighting, doesn't quit, perseveres, and ensures completion at all costs.

The Machine is known for getting sh!t done. They keep moving forward despite signs pointing them in a different direction or red flags indicating to stop. They tend to dominate and bulldoze, stick to the plan, achieve at all costs, and carry on regardless. They are often singularly attentive with blinders on and a "my way or the highway" mindset. But wait, isn't that how people achieve great things, by pushing through difficulties? Yes and no. Yes, being determined and prioritized on goals is incredibly important, BUT it needs to be done consciously and intentionally, not done via fear-based autopilot (we'll get into how to flip that switch in the next chapter).

The Machine holds on to the belief that "if I just keep going, it will be OK in the end" and uses action to control situations and perceptions. The Machine will not have a Plan B (or is not willing to implement it) and refuses to change course regardless of the circumstances. The

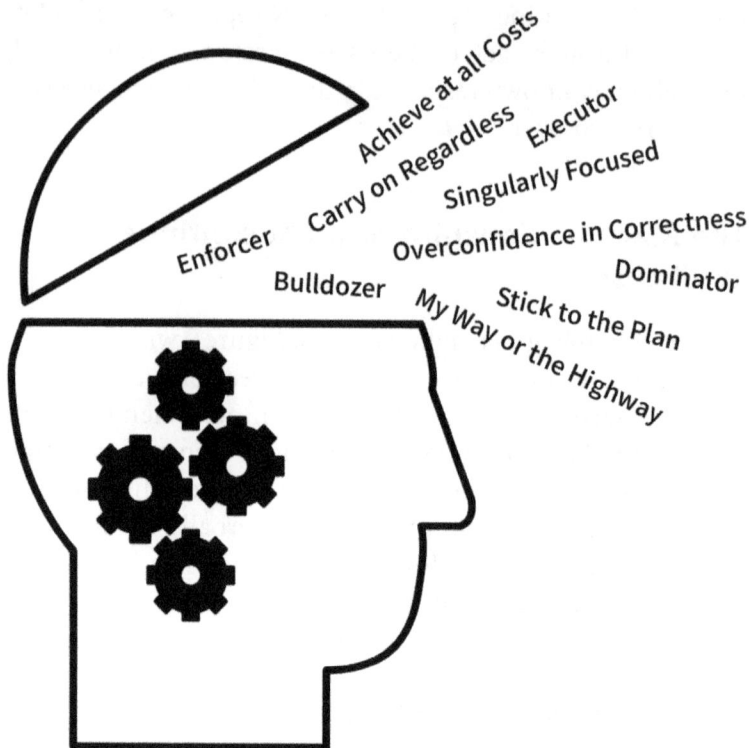

Figure 10   The Machine Conspirator

Machine may discuss, review, and evaluate many plans and many options, but once a decision is made, they find it difficult to divert or change course from that decision. They may see a possibility of another plan, but quitting is seen as a weakness, one that might make them look bad. The Machine will feel like they have to see something through – just to make sure they did absolutely everything they could in the situation. They may perceive that something could be seen as less of a failure if they do absolutely everything before quitting.

The Machine may make great progress initially. However, when the eventual plateau comes, the Machine works harder, refuses to accept the lack of progress, and digs in with a "just do it, at all costs" mentality.

The law of diminishing returns tells us that after a certain point, extra input produces a decreasing rate of output. It might even reach a point of negative returns, where the return isn't just smaller with additional investment, but it begins to decrease. When we reach this point, we get less out of something than we put in. Whether it's a new skill, a job, or in love, the Machine may sacrifice progress in the long run for success in the short run. Much like Boxer the Horse in George Orwell's *Animal Farm* whose answer to every problem and setback is "I will work harder," the Machine has embraced the response "I will work harder" to address failures, stress, and mistakes.[1] In *Animal Farm*, Boxer eventually collapses from overwork. The Machine, like Boxer, works harder and longer in response to failure and may even see burnout as a badge of honor.

With a warrior's façade as their armor against the ever-present threat of being cast aside or judged harshly for their insecurities and inadequacies, Machines are constantly reinforcing the idea that stopping, pivoting, and/or asking for help is a significant threat to their sense of self and who they want others to believe they are. Showing this sort of "weakness" is not an option for the Machine. We might hear the Machine leading the charge with "damn the torpedoes, full speed ahead" regardless of the risks or dangers. Because of the Machine Conspirator's singular commitment to accomplishment, they may find it impossible to pivot from or quit an undertaking, decision, or direction. This will result in an inability to hear or listen to advice from coaching or guidance from others. If learning something new requires failure, mistakes, or errors, then this Conspirator isn't willing to take this chance. There's a loss of face that comes with failing when adjusting course means admitting failure.

The word quit is not in the Machine's vocabulary; they refuse to quit even when it's clear a course correction is required. We've all known someone like this (or maybe that someone is us). The directions don't seem right, we've been driving in circles, and yet we can't stop and ask for directions. Keeley and her family went into Machine mode even though the GPS map had them on a dirt road in the middle of nowhere two-tracking in a minivan on terrain unsuitable for a mountain goat. This is the Conspirator who was in the driver seat of Noël's fateful bike race. Noël's Machine Conspirator pushed her to keep going in the bike ride, regardless of the pain. When Melisa was a teen, her mother yelled that she never finished anything. This perception of a failure from her mother made it impossible for Melisa not to finish – even books that she hated.

The Flight Conspirator: the Magician's masterful escape from failure

Moving to the upper left quadrant of Figure 9 is the Magician at the intersection of active and avoid: the flight response to failure or threat of failure. The Magician is a cagy, slippery obfuscator. The Magician can slip out of any sticky situation. They can rationalize, justify, sugarcoat, and obscure just about any situation. The Magician Conspirator regularly flees from difficult situations as a protective means because the threat of confronting these situations head on is perceived to be far greater than just avoiding them altogether.

The Magician makes excuses for failures. Nothing is ever the Magician's fault, and they can find an excuse for anything. Escaping responsibility is their forte. The Magician might affectionately be known as "Ms or Mr Wrong, But…" because they are likely to have the "I was wrong, but [fill in the blank]" defense for failure. The Magician might have a timeframe

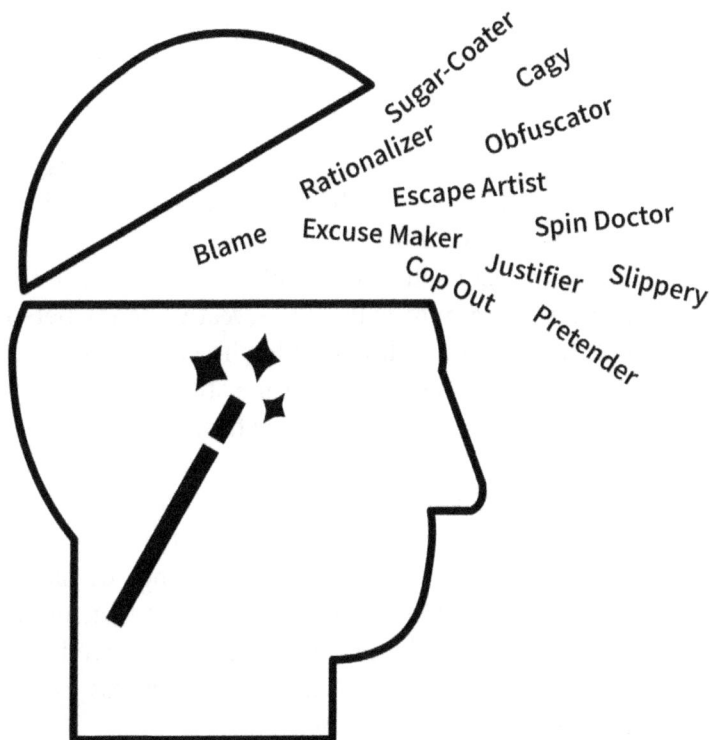

Figure 11   The Magician Conspirator

defense, "but wait until next year," the near-miss defense, "but only by a little," or the out-of-left-field defense, "but who would have seen that coming?" The other defense might be the "better safe than sorry" defense where the "but" is "but I was almost right."[2] Essentially, the Magicians blame anything but themselves for a failed outcome. The Magician Conspirator may not even be able to see their true failure because they are so involved in the excuses they are making. They spend time theorizing about the cause of the failure rather than truly thinking or reflecting about what went wrong. These excuse

makers are truly creative with justifications rather than allowing their fallibility to drive self-reflection. For the Magician,
it might look like they are reflecting but they are really justifying their own mistakes. This Conspirator may begin with:
"Look, I'm not trying to justify what happened, I just want to
explain it"… only to realize… that they are simply justifying
the path they took and/or decisions made.

The Magician Conspirator will often cast blame with a
wide net entangling anything from the weather to the person
seated next to them to technology to the circumference of
the Earth. The Magician Conspirator may blame bad luck for
failures or see them as the result of external circumstances
(if only the stock hadn't crashed, if only the customer placed
a different order, if only Betty Sue had done her part). They
conspire to shift responsibility or escape it altogether by
shifting the blame to people, actions, or things outside of
their control. On the other hand, the Magician Conspirator
doesn't see how luck (random chance) may have played a role
in their success as well. Instead, they credit success to their
inherent abilities or skills.

Another manifestation of the Magician Conspirator may
show up as overconfidence. Overconfidence bias has them
believe that they don't need to change anything that they
are doing. They are self-assured because of their successes.
They jump in and assume that all will turn out well regardless of their level of preparation (if they prepare at all). They
may know the right way to prepare for the event, but their
overconfidence entices them to choose the easy way. Once
they spin the outcome as "not so bad," learning from their
mistakes becomes very difficult. They struggle with taking
responsibility for the process, independent of the outcome,
thus lack a realistic view of what is required to be successful.
In the end, they always have excuses for any outcome that
doesn't turn out well.

When the Magician Conspirators are skilled and aware,
they are very efficient problem solvers. However, as they

develop habits or routines around their daily work, they revert to autopilot resulting in them being less aware. This lack of awareness can quickly become an obstacle leading to failure when novel situations requiring creative solutions present themselves. There is a term in psychology for this manifestation of the Magician Conspirator: The Dunning-Kruger Effect.[3] David Dunning and Justin Kruger found that the overconfident, those who "grossly overestimated" their actual performance, were really "unskilled and unaware." Pilots and surgeons, both highly trained professionals, are examples of professions susceptible to this failure response. One research study found that their errors tend not to be on the first or second surgery or flight but the fifteenth – just when they have begun to gain confidence.

The Magician may treat failure like Voldemort in the Harry Potter books: "He who shall not be named."[4] In other words, if we don't call it a failure, it's not. There is some sleight of hand regarding failure with the Magician Conspirator: once they can explain the mistake, *POOF* it is no longer a mistake. Bioethicist Nancy Berlinger, in her 2005 book on medical error, *After Harm*, describes the way denial is perpetuated with medical doctors.[5] "Observing more senior physicians, students learn that their mentors and supervisors believe in, practice, and reward the concealment of errors," Berlinger wrote. "They learn how to talk about unanticipated outcomes until a 'mistake' morphs into a 'complication.' Above all, they learn not to tell the patient anything." Berlinger goes on to describe "the depth of physicians' resistance to disclosure and the lengths to which some will go to justify the habit of nondisclosure – it was only a technical error, things just happen, the patient won't understand, the patient does not need to know."

All three of us have had our share of Magician Conspirator situations. Melisa's Magician Conspirator shows up when trying to learn to speak a foreign language. Her fear of "looking bad" (saying a word incorrectly) has her not even try to speak to others but secretly she practices with language apps.

She still struggles with this particular Conspirator. Keeley's medical school exam is an example where she blamed a "stupidly difficult test" on the less than stellar outcome rather than looking at her lack of studying as a possible cause. Noël started a business which failed to thrive. She blamed her failure on the world situation at the time (COVID). You can see how there might be a sliver of truth in all of this blame. This is exactly where a Magician works their magic: by exploiting half-truths and converting them into the truth, the whole truth, and nothing but the truth.

The Statue Conspirator's freeze response will show up as indecisive and hesitant behavior

In the lower left windowpane of Figure 9, where passivity and avoidance intersect, sits the Statue Conspirator. The autopilot or Emotional Hijack for a Statue may take on several forms due to the paralyzing nature of fear. They are often frozen and unable to move in any direction, showing up as indecisive, stuck in analysis paralysis, or as a procrastinator. The Statue Conspirator may also dabble in a bit of everything but never fully committing or quitting before a failure occurs.

The Statue Conspirator may continue to postpone starting something until it's either almost too late or too late for the event to be successful. This Conspirator is not likely to see themselves procrastinating and therefore is often self-sabotaging. The Emotional Hijack of a Statue Conspirator may look like a fence-sitter. Imagine sitting on a fence, looking at either side of the wide-open land all around. We can see what's happening on both sides of the fence, but we can't experience it, we cannot move anything forward on either side. We aren't in the action and we convince ourselves that from our perch we are safe from the consequences of those actions. The Statue may judge those on either side of the fence for taking action and may be able to see problems, defects, or

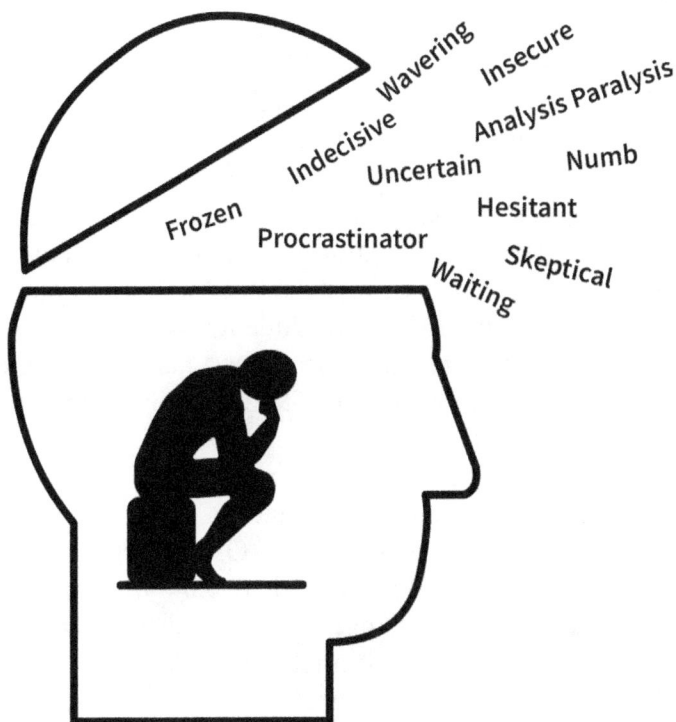

Figure 12   The Statue Conspirator

failures but they themselves have an *incomplete perspective* because they are not *in* the action. They may think of failure and success as *either/or*, which limits their view further.

Another expression of the Statue Conspirator's indecisiveness might be as a dabbler. Indecision can feel less daunting than choosing one side or the other, bouncing from thing to thing like a pinball, dabbling in everything, never committing to anything. In this expression, the Statue loves starting things but repeatedly fails to finish, especially when things begin to get difficult or routine. We might hear the Statue say or act "If I can't win, I won't play." Sadly, the Statue will dabble in many things but will not stick to anything long enough to develop a sufficient level of skill. The Statue Conspirator may overvalue performance and undervalue experience; they are concerned about being experts and performing so it is not OK to just finish, to just experience, or to enjoy. They cannot misstep or be second best, the fear of failing is too great. Statues can develop reputations as quitters or dilettantes. They are excited and passionate about the initial potential but rapidly lose interest and conclude it wasn't their passion after all, especially after they encounter a hardship or unexpected hurdle. As a dabbler, the Statue can't learn and grow from failures because they freeze to protect themselves from experiencing failure in the first place.

Another manifestation of the Statue Conspirator is being the ultimate avoider, like an ostrich (OK, an ostrich doesn't really do this, but they are fabled to bury their heads in the sand at any sign of danger). They tend to avoid information when they suspect it might be unpleasant, even if it might help in achieving their goals. By staying in the known they keep themselves safe from the ominous threat of the unknown. Avoiding information because we suspect it might be bad is a very human reaction. Professor Ayelet Fishbach has researched motivation and negative feedback. Fishbach's laboratory found that "when failure threatens the ego, people disengage from the failed experience and stop paying attention."[6] When the Statue Conspirator is faced with the discomfort of negative emotions, they stop paying attention and will avoid information that might bring on further negative feelings. As humans, we are naturally inclined to avoid failure more than we innately pursue success. While this may be true for most of us, the Statue is especially prone to avoid failure and is willing to risk missing out on the possibility of great success to do so.

The Statue Conspirators often experience high levels of worry as if danger is lurking around every corner, poised to strike like a T-rex if it even senses motion. They may appear hesitant, skeptical, wavering, or insecure. Consistency is safe. Change is unsafe.

Melisa found herself acting as a Statue when she reflected on her father's death. For a year she knew that something wasn't working but was frozen with fear of facing the grief and loss of her father head on. She knew it wasn't right, but the familiar often feels safer than the unknown. There were so very many unknowns involved if she were to deal with his death that she stayed frozen like a statue for a year. Keeley had a similar experience after receiving the results of her MCAT. The laser job was familiar and relatively safe compared to the unknown outcome of studying and taking the test again. Noël had a Statue Conspirator experience while writing this book. She wanted to quit. She stewed in her misery but couldn't bring herself to talk to anyone about her feelings nor could she bring herself to quit. After weeks of living in this miserable state, she forced herself to talk about what was going on. Being a statue feels safe because you are not actively choosing a potential wrong path, you're staying in familiar territory. But familiarity doesn't always mean safety, much like the unknown doesn't always mean danger. When we are frozen in our fear-based autopilot, we cannot see the danger in the familiar or the safety in the unknown and find it nearly impossible to see that taking action, especially conscious action, can open the door to previously unimagined possibilities for growth and connection.

The Satellite Conspirator is the consummate follower and peacekeeper

Finally, the fourth quadrant of Figure 9 is the passive controller, the fawning response to failure or the threat of failure that we've named the Satellite Conspirator. You might also think of the Satellite as a people-pleasing follower.

The gravity of groups or dominating individuals keeps the Satellite Conspirator orbiting on a path of others' choosing, not their own. Not wanting to rock the boat and risk being thrown overboard, the Satellite can fall victim to paying more attention to the needs of others and ignore their own needs. Satellites are notorious people pleasers intent on keeping the peace of others often at the expense of their own internal peace. There can be a significant lack of self-confidence or lack of trust in themselves to make the right decision or take the next right step, so they rely on others for direction.

The Satellite Conspirator may be described as a conformist: whatever everyone else is doing, they will do. "Fifty Million Frenchmen Can't Be Wrong" was a popular hit song in 1929 written by Cole Porter, which compared the political climate in the United States (censorship and prohibition) to the free thinkers in Paris.[7] The argument that "if everyone is doing it, it must be a good idea."

The Satellite's mistakes or failures are often because they follow what others are doing even if they suspect it's not the right thing. This type of Conspirator will copy other people's choice, even when they don't know how the other person's motives, values, or preferences reflect or compare to their own. The Satellite would rather look good by conforming rather than risk standing out because of their decisions.

The Satellite Conspirator can be difficult to spot. Noël experienced being a Satellite with a friend in high school. Noël's best friend's mother was an unacknowledged alcoholic. Everyone, including Noël, looked the other way as this woman's behavior became more and more destructive over time. When she was younger, Melisa would find herself following the in-crowd to bars or late-night activities even though she hated it. She wanted to fit in, and everyone else seemed to have such a good time. However, she found herself miserable and tired the next day. The energy spent was not worth the evening out. Feeling out of her element in the business world of lasers, much of Keeley's career unfolded due to her Satellite Conspirator.

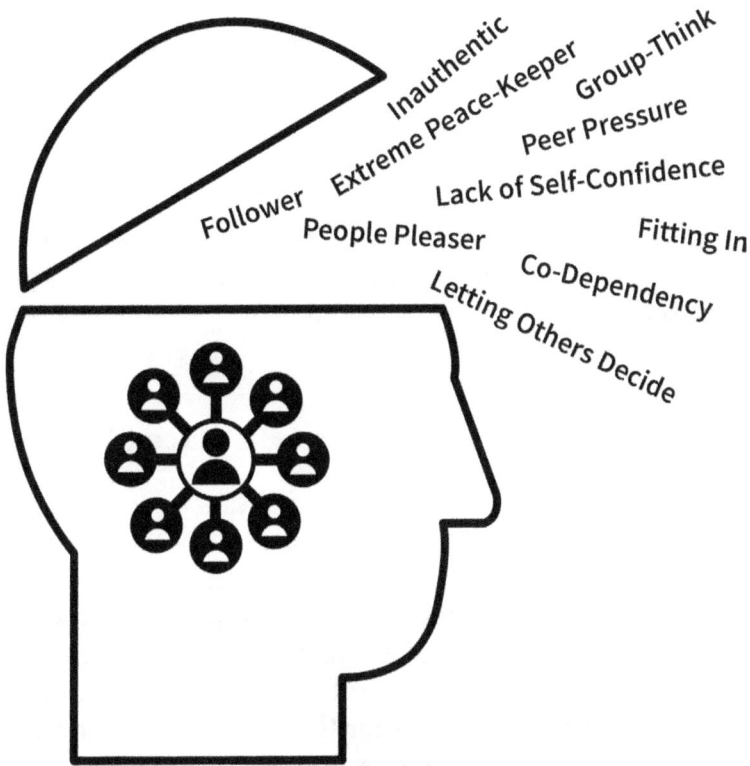

Figure 13   The Satellite Conspirator

Keeley's story

After joining the laser industry, my career path quickly turned into a Satellite. With a false narrative that I was an outsider due to my lack of formal engineering education, I was constantly in fear of being discovered as a fraud at the slightest misstep. Every time the company I worked for downsized or restructured, I was asked to take on vastly different roles that had little to no correlation with my current role. As people left the company or as the company expanded, I was asked to take on additional responsibilities and pivot in ways that still baffle me to this day. Never did I reject these requests or even push back. Occasionally, I even actively worked to find justifications for why this new role/responsibility was a good fit! I didn't look at my growing resume and seek out positions that filled me with excitement. I simply took whatever role was presented to me and ran with it.

Conspirators are reacting from a place of fear

Conspirators are not inherently bad or always wrong, they are simply reacting from a place of fear to a type of threat. Recall from Part 1, there are three primary threats. The following table illustrates an example of a mistaken premise that each Conspirator might hold, and the threat experienced as a result.

When we react from a place of fear, our primary goal is to regain a sense of safety and security and get back to our comfort zone by whatever means necessary. We know that we are not learning and growing in our comfort zone, so getting out of that zone is what we must do if we ever want to ease the heavy burden that failure forces us to carry.

Table 2   Premise matrix

Conspirator	Primary threat	Mistaken premise
Machine	Safety/security	I am what I accomplish.
Magician	Safety/security	No failure here.
Statue	Safety/security	If I don't address it, it isn't a problem.
Satellite	Belonging	Conflict is not worth the trouble.

Our Conspirators may be a pattern

When we reflect on our failures, we can often find patterns of our fear responses emerging. We call the Conspirator that shows up repeatedly our Usual Suspect. After much soul-searching with different failures over the time the three of us worked on this book, we discovered that we had experienced all Conspirators, but that each of us also had a different Usual Suspect depending on the circumstances of the failure. When it came to Keeley's personal life, she often found herself in Statue mode, unable to make choices, stuck in analysis paralysis until forced by external factors into action, not wanting to rock the boat no matter how turbulent the waters were. When it came to her kids, however, watch out: Keeley's Machine showed up in full battle gear ready to throw hands with anyone and anything that dared mess with her family. Logic and reason were thrown forcefully out the window: fight now and ask questions later. For Keeley and her career, she was often in Satellite mode adapting to whatever the company needed. Once in a new role or saddled with more responsibilities, she then flipped to the Machine mode to work harder and power through regardless of changing circumstances; sleep be damned, doing all that she could to control the perception of others by proving she belonged there.

Once we have reacted in one of our autopilot conspirator modes, we limit ourselves to further conspiratory reactions if we don't consciously interrupt that cycle. Melisa failed to get a much-anticipated promotion and went into the Magician mode immediately following the news. The story didn't end with her stuck in Magician-style blame because Melisa's most common Conspirator (aka her Usual Suspect) is a Machine and once her Magician flipped inward, she quickly jumped on the Machine train and charged full steam ahead with additional readings, trainings, and certifications convincing herself that if she just did a little more, "they" wouldn't be able to reject her or cast her aside again and she could keep herself "safe" from the pain that situation inflicted.

Noël discovered her Usual Suspect Conspirator is the Machine. She tends to charge ahead and needs to prove her worth and abilities by doing things for herself. She's very independent – to a fault at times. While writing this book, Noël went through a period of getting stuck, feeling like a failure, and wanting to quit. She can't remember ever wanting to quit something so badly as she wanted to quit writing this book. She was initially powering through as usual, but then began not meeting agreed upon writing deadlines, couldn't find her unique voice or contribution to the writing, had surgery on a finger that was impacting her physical ability to write, and worried about everything she wrote not being perfect enough. She flipped from Machine to Statue and was ready to throw in the towel refusing to do anything else. Fortunately, she was able to work through her issue and didn't let either the Machine or the Statue Conspirators fully take over. More about that process in the next chapter.

It is unlikely that we have only one conspirator type as an unconscious response to the failures in our lives. We may have a dominant type, but different failures may create emotional responses consistent with more than one conspirator type. It's important that we all look carefully, so we don't miss opportunities to see other autopilot responses that may be at play in our lives. These Conspirators can be sneaky little buggers!

By learning the wrong lesson, we can get stuck with a Life Sentence

When we cannot move beyond past mistakes and/or decisions we've made, we are destined to repeat those or similar missteps. We may have learned the "wrong" lesson from a failure and incorporated that lesson into a false belief that may have been appropriate as a child or young adult but no longer serves us. As a result, we may unwittingly find our-selves living out a Life Sentence – which dooms us to a repeti-tive conspirator pattern throughout our lives.[8]

After failing an exam or set of exams, we may begin to think "I'm not a math person" or "I can't spell." Struggling to spell in third grade doesn't mean that as an adult we can't be a Scrabble champ. In these examples, we feel that what happens is out of our control. Too many times, faulty beliefs like "I'm not good at math" or worse are issued in child-hood and can quickly morph into Life Sentences. Melisa's response to her embarrassing failures in attempting to speak words in different languages that she wasn't familiar with how to pronounce, was to internalize the failure, stop trying, and blame herself. Her takeaway was that she wasn't good at languages. By virtue of Melisa avoiding the discomfort of that failure, not investing the time to understand exactly what happened or gain perspective through self-reflection, she essentially learned the wrong lesson and internalized a false belief that she carried with her for most of her life. After her mother's *one* comment about not finishing, Melisa handed herself another Life Sentence. She couldn't quit things. By uncovering this pattern, Melisa was finally able to create a "Didn't Finish" folder in her Goodreads account to hold books she didn't enjoy. The "Didn't Finish" folder is now up to 22 titles over the last six years. These types of Life Sentences are issued from a fixed mindset. We lean into these failures and look for confirmation around us that the Life Sentence is true rather than embracing a growth mind-set and saying "When I was eight years old, I failed a math test. That doesn't mean anything about my math compe-tency at 20." The good news about Life Sentences, much like our Conspirators, is that once we can see them for what they are, we have the ability to free ourselves from their powerful grasp.

Tripping Hazards are the gap between expectations and reality

This chapter may seem very discouraging since our Conspirators seem to automatically take control when we feel threatened and faced with the possibility of failure. We likely have a Usual Suspect Conspirator who dominates over all the others and we're starting to see patterns that can be especially painful to acknowledge. If we learned the wrong lesson at some point in our lives, we may have also discovered that we unknowingly created a Life Sentence for ourselves. Ouch. If that's where you are now, that's good news: awareness is the first step to recovery. Once we start to see patterns with our failure Conspirators (recognizing what's going on behind the scenes, so to speak), we can take a step back and zoom in on the Tripping Hazards that set us up for our conspirator responses in the first place. The Tripping Hazard we have found to be consistently present in all of our biggest Faceplants resulted from a disconnect between our expected outcomes and what happened in any given situation. If we look at our expectations versus outcomes as displayed in Figure 14, three scenarios are possible. When our expectation matches the outcome, we carry on without much fanfare or afterthought. When our expectation is less than the outcome, we chalk it up to great luck or pat ourselves on the back. When our expectation is greater than the actual outcome, we view this as a failure.

Expectations are a natural part of our humanity. Expectations are what we think the future will look like based on our beliefs and assumptions. Our expectations flavor the way we see the world, shape our beliefs, guide our actions and, more importantly, our reactions. We have expectations in all areas of our lives from our personal relationships to our career objectives. Understanding where our expectations come from can be helpful. Our expectations come from a mishmash of contributing factors that, once we see them, can be grounded in reality and significantly more aligned with

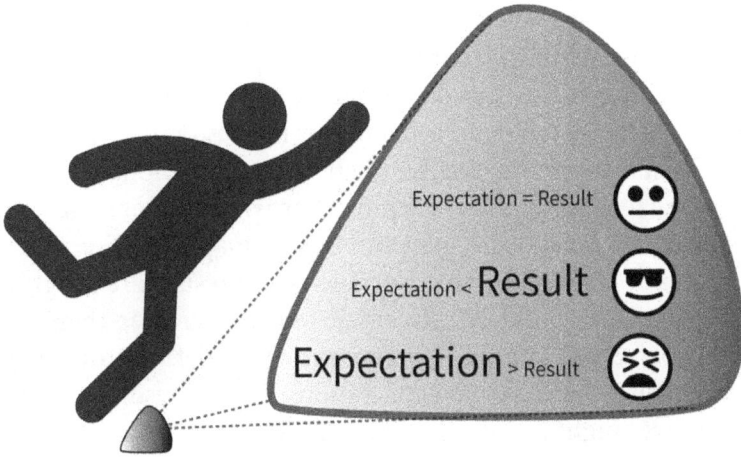

Figure 14   Expectation disconnect

possible outcomes, thus reducing the disconnect. Societal norms and family of origin play huge roles in building our expectations. Previous experiences and knowledge add layers upon layers to those expectations as well. Our hopes, dreams, and perceived impact on others are often not matched by reality and further inflate our expectations by creating a fantasy world where we are the hero. With all of these factors coming into play, the expectations we build are as unique as the individuals who carry them.

Expectation disconnect is the main Tripping Hazard that leads to our Faceplants, but some of those downfalls have a significantly greater impact than others. The perceived severity of a failure is a function of the impact the failure will have and how much we care about the failure. The equation below illustrates this relationship:

$$Impact \times Care = Severity$$

The greater the span of impact (on things like time, money, and people) and/or the greater the level of care (a whim versus a life's mission), the greater the perceived severity of a failure. Trip when you're walking alone (not usually a big deal), versus trip in front of your friends (embarrassing but survivable), versus trip on a stage in front of an audience of people you are trying to influence or impress (game over!).

When there is a gap between our expectations and the results (reality) of what is achieved or what happens, we can experience several different feelings or maybe even a roller coaster of feelings. If the expectations and results are roughly the same, or if the results are better and greater than we anticipated, we might feel happiness, joy, relief. On the other hand, when we have big expectations and the results are less than, we might feel disappointment, frustration, sadness, or depression. We might even feel that our whole view of reality has been rocked to the core. This is called cognitive dissonance.[9] Cognitive dissonance is the mental discomfort we experience when there is a discrepancy between our expectations, beliefs, values, or feelings and reality or results.

Tripping Hazards can be internally or externally driven

One of the most obvious internal Tripping Hazards is trying something new; in other words, being a rookie. There will naturally be a lot of failure as a rookie. The rookie may have some expectations of failure, but a pervasive or prolonged failure is not something we usually plan on. (This of the downward plunge in the learning curve model from Part 1.) External Tripping Hazards often come from societal focus and celebration of early achievement. We see examples of 12-year-olds graduating from college or tech bros making their first million by the age of 22, and we feel like a failure because we haven't achieved those milestones.

The rookie doesn't typically have prior experience or history with whatever they are attempting. As a result, they have a limited or lack of understanding of the complexities of the undertaking. They should expect to make a lot of mistakes and fail a lot, but because rookies don't know what they don't know, they can overestimate their abilities and underestimate the challenge. We have all been in this boat. It is difficult to pick up a new skill as we get older. Think about learning chess at 40 with your 10-year-old who is learning like a sponge or picking up pickleball with your 15-year-old. The 10-year-old chess beginner and the 15-year-old pickleball beginner may be able to pick up these skills much faster than an adult learner. The first attempt at anything new results in either a step or misstep. The missteps can drive us to be more determined to succeed the next time (perseverance) or drive us to walk away with a commitment to never do this again (quit). We typically think of toddlers as the ultimate rookies. They will fail over and over until they crawl, then walk, then run. They do not feel any shame. They are rewarded with our accolades and pride. At some point, though, as a society, we (parents, teachers, politicians, companies) become obsessed with early achievers. We compare notes on when our child takes their first steps and speaks their first word. We learn that demonstrating skill competence earlier is better. In Noël's work as a career counselor to undergraduate students, most students are new to searching for internships and full-time professional roles after graduating from college. Students are rookies at writing resumes, having networking conversations, and negotiating job offers – to name a few.

Mistakes/failures are often made during various steps of the job search/internship process as students learn. Some common examples are not getting a resume critiqued by a professional before applying for a job or going about networking conversations in an ineffective manner. These mistakes can result in missed employment opportunities. When we've been doing things for a long time, we can forget how daunting it can be to do something for the first time. Noël is constantly reminded by her students of the courage it takes to do something new and face the rejection that often goes hand in hand with searching for a job.

One of the most important aspects of being a rookie is to repeat the practice–fail–reflect cycle, to continue learning and growing. Noël stresses this with her students by encouraging them to try a new approach with their resume, send a different type of message to a potential networking contact, and concentrate on upcoming opportunities, not belabor what has passed. In other words, don't allow the failure to define the student's job search process going forward. Encourage them to move on and not get stuck in the emotion of the failure.

Being a rookie, whether attempting something new early in life or late in life, can be a great experience. At the same time, it can also be frustrating not to be able to pick something up quickly. Keeping our expectations for success grounded in reality – especially when we hit the challenging bottom of the learning curve – can better position us to navigate our rookie phases.

One of the most common external Tripping Hazards manifests as the late bloomer.[10] Late bloomers are the opposite of an early achiever. The late bloomer is a person whose talents and interests only become publicly evident later in life. It's easy to find plenty of stories of famous people who started art or writing later in life; yet they had previously shown no particular aptitude for these skills. The late bloomer may be the person who takes time off between high school and college or does not complete either one until later in life. It is probably not too much of a stretch to say that late bloomers' talents and capabilities may be completely invisible in their early life. As a result, the late bloomer may feel that they are an imposter or have failed because they compare themselves to the expectations of others.

Perfectionism can be a nagging Tripping Hazard for all Conspirators

Perfectionism is another case where expectations can go awry. What perfect looks like is different for everyone.

With perfection being rooted in perception it is essentially unobtainium – something that does not exist and cannot be achieved, but that doesn't stop us from trying. There may be times when striving for excellence is good and the outcome produced is amazing. The danger is when striving for excellence goes to an extreme and morphs into perfectionism. Perfectionism is a self-destructive response to not being flawless or perfect. Perfectionists want to be seen as competent and accepted in the eyes of others, so they may spend their time getting everything "just so." The perfectionist has something to prove not just to those around them but also to themselves. There can be a deep-seated fear associated with not being perfect.

There are several ways perfectionism can present itself and keep us stuck. Perfection may keep us stuck in analysis paralysis. We can't make a decision; we are wavering and insecure about choosing a direction because we need to choose the *right* direction. We feel there must be a right way – if we just think about it long enough. This may lead to not completing projects or responding to people on time because the goal is focused on getting something perfect. Perfectionism may convince us to tweak and tweak something until it is perfect, causing us to spin in dizzyingly painful circles for fear of being judged as less than. For the perfectionist, nothing is ever quite good enough, and they are never satisfied. Perfectionism can also show up as powering through. The perfectionist may be exhausted, overwhelmed, depleted, and discouraged (burnout), but they must keep moving regardless. Perfectionists may be praised for their hard work, dedication, and accomplishments, but their need for perfection takes a toll on them. The failures of the perfectionist may not be seen or experienced by others as failures and may even be considered a success. This praise feeds the perfectionist's need for external validation, keeping the perfectionistic cycle in place.

Perfectionism tells us the story that "if I'm perfect, I will be safe from rejection," so our brains push us onward working diligently to protect our carefully crafted image. Perfection is a self-imposed and self-destructive conspiracy that prevents learning and growth by setting the bar at an impossible height, keeping us stuck with a huge Expectation Disconnect, ever critical of ourselves and others.

The Emotional Hijack response can be amplified

In Part 1, we discussed the three key threats that initiate our core fear responses: threats to self, threats to belonging, and threats to our safety/security. Each of the Conspirators has a primary fear that triggers them, but our Conspirators are all also subject to Amplifiers of those triggers.

Amplifiers are the other factors that alter our perceptions of failures. In Figure 15, we have identified three primary amplification factors: comparison, isolation, and lifequakes.

The Comparison Amplifier forces you to look at your situation in relation to others... "Bob is already CEO at age 35, I'm *just* a manager at 40." Comparing ourselves to others puts blinders on us and only allows us to see a carefully curated representation of the others' successes, blocking out the struggles and failures along their path, limiting our big picture view. The Isolation Amplifier tricks us into feeling alone in our struggle and ashamed to share it with others... "I'm so overwhelmed at work/school, but I can't tell anyone, or they will know I don't belong here." Isolation tricks us into believing we are the only one facing this challenge and it's better to hide it than to reveal it and risk the shock and harsh judgment of others. Lifequake Amplifiers seemingly come out of nowhere, jar us, make us feel as if our whole world is unstable, and upend our way of life... like Ian's cheating partner. Lifequakes force us to come face to face with our expectations and can make us question who we really are at our core. These Amplifiers intensify our feelings surrounding

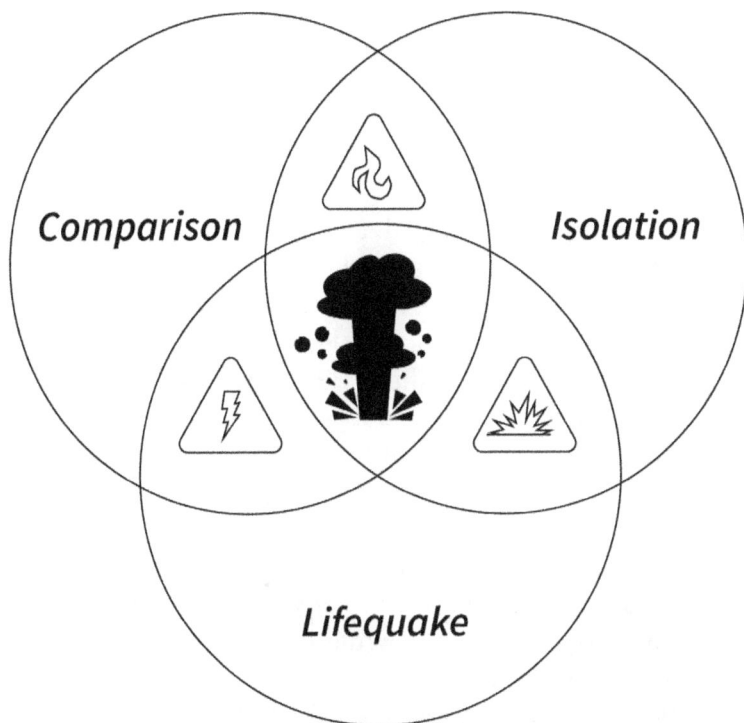

Figure 15   Amplifiers

failure individually by adding more and more fuel to our failure dumpster fire. They can also combine forces to not just
add extra fuel but also fan the flames expanding the ripple
effect of failure ever outward. With the three of them acting
in concert it can make our whole world feel like it is about to
implode.

This layering of Amplifiers was exactly what Noël experienced when she faced an overwhelming desire to quit writing
this book. When she reflected on this experience, she realized as time went on that the Statue Conspirator was at play.
This Conspirator's threat to safety and security got amplified.

Based on Figure 15, Noël's reaction to working on the book involved all three Amplifiers:

Noël's story

1. **Comparison:** I started comparing my writing to Melisa's and Keeley's. Melisa's super-power is her effectiveness at laying out the scaffolding of concepts in writing. She's also very well read. If a book has been published on failure, Melisa has read it! Keeley's brain works in mysterious ways. She has the ability to visualize processes and create pictures to illustrate them, plus she's hilarious and can write in a personal way without filters. Her writing is very conversational. When she writes she's able to express what goes on in my brain with her words. I couldn't find my voice. Everything I wrote seemed boring, useless, and uninspired.
2. **Isolation:** For several weeks, I didn't share that I was struggling and wanted to quit. I didn't share how I was having trouble finding my voice. I kept it to myself and felt isolated, overwhelmed, sad, and guilty for not getting the work done.
3. **Lifequake:** On top of that, I was having a series of medical procedures over several weeks. Even though they were planned, I did not anticipate how bad I was going to feel, or how significantly these procedures were going to inconvenience my everyday life for much longer than I expected.

With all these Amplifiers piling on, it's no wonder our autopilot Conspirators jump into action so quickly as the snowball barrels down the mountain towards us. All is not lost, however, as our body often warns us that we are about to be crushed by an avalanche of Expectation Disconnects and their Amplifier partners moments before our Conspirators take control. We can feel the rumble as our pulse quickens, breathing becomes shallow, face heats up, palms get sweaty, and our stomach summersaults away from us. Our bodies may also sense a change in gravity seemingly pulling us downward, making everything heavy and lethargic as if we're swimming upstream in pudding. These bodily sensations happen in the tiny space between our failure stimulus and our autopilot conspirator responses. By tuning into these red flags our body is waving for us, we can start to interrupt our autopilot reactions and shift into conscious decisions surrounding our actions, which is exactly what we will tackle in the next chapter.

TL;DR

- Conspirators are an autopilot response to a stimulus (perceived threat). The Conspirators are in control, and we aren't consciously making the decisions about our actions. The four primary responses are fight, flight, freeze, or fawn.
- An Emotional Hijack brings out our Conspirators. The Machine Conspirator, our fight response, has us charge ahead at all costs. The Magician Conspirator, our flight response, will make excuses, justify or sugarcoat events to escape responsibility. The Statue Conspirator, our freeze response, will be indecisive, be hesitant, and just wait for it to blow over. The Satellite Conspirator, our fawn response, is the consummate follower and peacekeeper.
- Our Conspirators tend to show up as a pattern in our lives. Our most prevalent or go-to Conspirator is our Usual Suspect.
- If we aren't careful, we could learn the wrong lesson and get stuck with a Life Sentence. A Life Sentence is an adopted view that we impose on ourselves, often unconsciously. If our Life Sentence is based on failure, we may find that we need to update our view.

- A Tripping Hazard is the result of an Expectation Disconnect – the gap between high expectations and lower than anticipated results. Cognitive dissonance is the mental discomfort we experience when there is a discrepancy between our beliefs, values, or feelings and reality or results. The incessant desire for perfection can be a nagging Tripping Hazard for all Conspirators. Starting with an unrealistic standard of perfection can easily lead to an Expectation Disconnect.
- Threats which initiate the Emotional Hijack can have additional factors that increase our reactions. Amplifiers of comparison, isolation, and lifequakes intensify the response of our Conspirators.

Where the rubber hits the road

In your journal, review your master failure list from the last chapter. There's a lot of material in this chapter to reflect on. Try as many exercises as possible before moving on.

- Review the list of failures in your past. Can you identify which Conspirator was in control of your reaction for each failure?
- After you've looked at your response to multiple failures, do you notice any patterns in your responses? Is there a Conspirator that shows up more than others? Do you have a Usual Suspect in different situations?
- For one of more of your failures, it may be helpful to do more digging into it. Analyze your response to these failures considering the conspiratorial responses. This may not be obvious, and you may need to spend time doing some expressive writing about your failure response. Ask four questions:
  1. What did we set out to do?
  2. What happened?
  3. Why did it happen?
  4. How did we respond?

- Look at your last week. What expectations did you have going into these situations? Were there any disconnects between your expectations and what happened?
- In looking at your failures, where did you feel the threat most – to your sense of self, to your belonging, or to your safety/security? Were there any Amplifiers that played a role in making the threat feel more intense?

Chapter 6

Explore your options

At this point, things can start to feel especially heavy. Discovering that we are on a fear-based conspirator hamster wheel can be particularly disheartening and make us question how we could be so foolish to not see these patterns sooner. But that's just it, these are the autopilot responses that our brain doesn't want us to see because this is how the brain tries to keep us in the familiar, keep us in the comfort zone, keep us "safe." Time for a heavy dose of self-compassion and embrace the "when we know better, we can do better" philosophy as we enter the *Explore* phase of the FREE model. This is the phase that will provide tangible ways that we can take this new knowledge and "do better." Not all methods will work for everyone. They will likely be somewhere on the sliding scale from "hard pass" to "meh" to "wow, that actually worked." The point of the *Explore* phase is to do just that, explore our options by taking them for a test drive.

In the last two chapters we saw how our Conspirators, those autopilot reactions that keep us from learning and growing from failure, keep us on a familiar path. While this may be how we've always responded to failures in the past, it doesn't have to determine our future. After the difficult time of reflection, it's time to set a course for self-improvement. We want to get ourselves back in the driver's seat of our own lives. In this chapter, we'll explore some tools that allow us to stay open to the inevitable failure and learn from these experiences. We'll also share some techniques that may allow

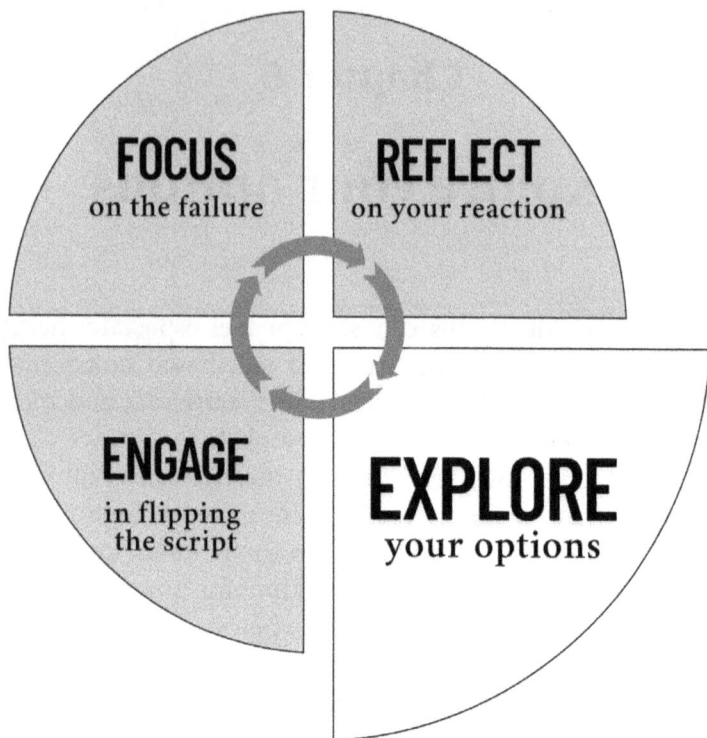

Figure 16   Explore your options

us to begin exploring other options by taking small steps and incorporating small changes. First, we'll need a new perspective on failure. Next, we must learn to spot a Tripping Hazard and interrupt a Conspirator before it becomes an Emotional Hijack – or as soon as we realize we are in the downward spiral. We will introduce the Liberators, the alter ego of the Conspirators, who set us free from these conspiracy paths and help us learn and grow. Liberators allow us to adjust those patterns that we found ourselves defaulting into and forge a new trail instead. After liberation, we can edit our own story and create a new paradigm for our future. In the last few sections of this chapter, we'll discuss some additional tools that can be used to avoid Tripping Hazards that we are aware of and learn to work around those surprise Tripping Hazards that catch us off guard.

Redefining failure gives us freedom from the past

As we begin the self-improvement phase of *hansei* and bring a fresh new perspective about failure to our lives, we can now create and update *our* personal definition of what failure means. It will not be easy but it's time to put the funk of emotions we associated with this failure behind us. In our past, failure was the end. We failed, period. We felt yucky. We made failure mean something negative and bad in our lives. Let's leave the "failure is the end of the world as we know it" definition behind. Rather than hiding or avoiding failure, let's take steps to become more resilient, build our failure immune system, and acknowledge that failures continue to happen to us all.

A new definition of failure can make a huge difference in our perception going forward, but we need to choose a new definition that works for us. We can choose to see failure as a gift that allows us to improve. Or our new definition can acknowledge that failure isn't the end of anything, it's a guide, a map, showing us the path that we are uniquely forging for our lives. Because we aren't given a map at birth with directions on what we should do and how we should do it, we must figure it out and create this guidebook for our own lives. We can assume the stance that failure is not an obstacle on the path but instead lays a solid foundation for the future.

No more does failure have to drag us into a funk or at least not for long. With our new definition of failure, we can see that failures highlight where we have more room to become our best selves through further growth and development. In this new definition, failure can be our *sensei*, our teacher, coach, and mentor. We can rewrite our failure stories considering our new definition of failure. Creating new definitions of failure without a means to implement them is just hot air without a balloon to help us soar. It's time to add some new tools to our quiver, so we are better equipped for whatever lies ahead.

Interrupting an Emotional Hijack is a first step toward freedom

"Between stimulus and response, there is a space.
In that space is our power to choose our response.
In our response lies our growth and our freedom."[1]

The "space" is the point where we can interrupt the Conspirators and their autopilot reactions and flip the script to conscious action. In that space lives a story, a hastily constructed, falsehood laden, mythical story, but a story, nonetheless. Our mind loves a good story, as a story helps us to make sense of the senseless, familiarity of the unfamiliar, and certainty of the unpredictable. Our mind is incredibly adept at creating stories and connections where none exist. It often uses malarky and serves up speculation as fact to keep us safe. And what is the best way our mind knows to keep us safe? Our mind creates a story so terrifying that it triggers our autopilot to get us the heck up on out of this precarious spot. Expanding that space allows us to inject a fact-checker into the story and choose a conscious action instead.

The first and simplest method for interrupting an Emotional Hijack is simply pausing and taking a breath or two to allow your brain to begin processing information. Tuning into our bodily reactions can be a great indicator that we are about to hit the slippery slope down into an autopilot response. Much like a warning light on our car's dashboard, when our pulse starts to quicken and our stomach sinks, our body is essentially waving red flags that danger (to our sense of self, our safety, and our connectedness) is lurking. Noticing our visceral reaction brings attention to that "space" so that we can extend it instead of jumping straight into our fear response. Taking a few deep breaths or practicing "4–4–4

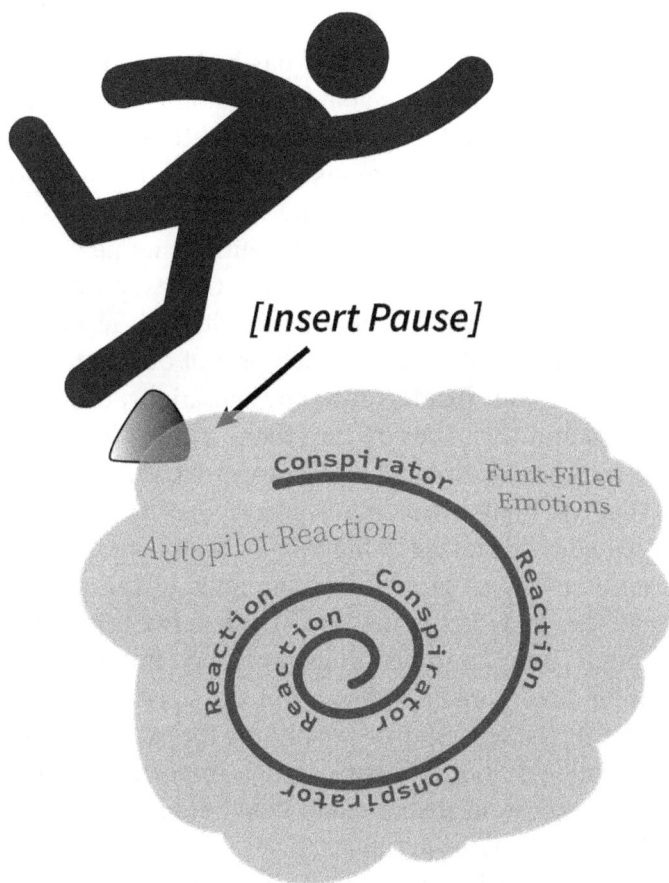

Figure 17   Pausing the conspirator spiral

breathing" (inhale to a count of four, hold for a count of four and exhale for a count of four) seems overly simplistic, but can work miracles in toning down our fear response and giving us a little more space to revise the story.

Practicing mindfulness is another great way to create space between our Tripping Hazards and Conspirators. (If you're rolling your eyes and thinking this is hippy-dippy stuff or crossing your arms in a been-there-done-that-I-can't-meditate posture, we'll spare you the lecture on all the brain science of the positive effects it can have.) We fully acknowledge the struggle is real *and* we know it is possible; Keeley has a mind like a pinball machine *and* has had a regular meditation practice for years. The goal here is not to inspire you to fly around the world to study with meditation masters or to convince you to live like a monk. The goal is to ground ourselves in the present reality instead of getting whisked away by our Conspirators. When implementing any new activity or new habit the key is to start small. One way to practice mindfulness is through a body scan. Starting at our toes, then bringing our attention to each part of our body, slowly working up to our head. Notice any sensations, discomfort, or tension and then breathe into those places. This can not only increase relaxation but also clue us in to more subtle red flags that our body is sending us in response to fear that we can use to our advantage in flipping the script going forward.

Another way to ground our thoughts in the present is through the "5–4–3–2–1 method." Look at five things, touch four things, listen to three things, smell two things and taste one thing. The number and order of the senses isn't important, mixing the senses up or not finding the exact right numbers isn't the point of this exercise. The important thing is to get *all* our senses in the here and now because the here and now is the only place we can act.

To try meditation, start small. There are some great apps that have free, beginner offerings to help guide us through the meditation process. When Keeley first started meditating, she couldn't even make it through two minutes without being completely derailed and following her thoughts down a rabbit hole or getting up and walking away. Emptying our minds completely is not possible, but not getting carried away by our thoughts can be done with practice; practice that will help us to increase our stamina for calm over time. Self-compassion in combination with the expectation that mindfulness is hard are both critical factors to make this work. On the day of writing Keeley sat down with an intention to meditate for 15 minutes with only ambient wave noise and single chimes to indicate the passage of time in 5-minute increments. When the first 5-minute chime sounded, she was absolutely astounded at how quickly and calmly the time had passed #nailedit... and then promptly got swept away by her disconnected freight train of thoughts until the next chime, oops... gentle redirect of her attention to her breath without berating the derailment helped get her back close to the calm of the first 5 minutes, though it seemed noticeably longer. So yeah, it's a process. A process that needs patience, persistence, and realistic expectations – much like the rest of life.

We can also use a physical cue to invoke a physical memory, creating an Emotional Reset Button.[2] This will be something we need to practice ahead of time. The first step is to choose a spot on our body that we can touch conveniently. Forehead between the eyes, chin, neck or throat, or palm are a few examples that you can use. (Melisa prefers touching her throat with her right index finger as her Emotional Reset Button. This is a physical cue not to let the Statue take over – to use her voice.) To create the Emotional Reset Button, touch this spot with your index finger and create a body memory of calm and peace. This calm state will be our emotional ground state. Establish what this feels like while alone and not stressed, anxious, or irritated. Practice touching this spot and recalling the peaceful feeling several times to further establish this emotional grounding. The more we practice the easier it becomes to get to this ground state. Another incredibly simple and incognito physical cue to avert our attention to the present is to rub the fingertips of our thumb and any finger together in a circular motion. Feel the fingerprints. (Rub any other skin on your hands and arms and it feels smooth but rub your thumb and finger together and it feels more like a windshield wiper skipping across a dry windshield. You just tried it, didn't you? Trippy right? Once you've tried it, it's hard to *not* feel your fingerprints when you rub your fingers together. Sorry, not sorry.)

Practicing initially in front of a mirror can be helpful; eventually we want to be our own mirror. We can observe ourselves going from a heightened emotional and physical state to a calm and peaceful state. We want to practice and practice until we can return to our ground state as quickly as possible. Psychiatrist Eric Berne has named the time it takes for us to return to our baseline ground state as the afterburn.[3] The time to recover will vary both physically and emotionally. In some cases, this may be fast and in other cases it may take minutes to hours, maybe even days depending on the threat. (If there is a situation where there has been prolonged exposure to threats, it is best to seek professional help.) One thing that is important to point out is that the sooner emotional regulation is achieved, the easier it will be and more successful we will be at minimizing the impact. We want to deal with the difficult emotions surrounding failure triggers before these emotions suck us down (or as soon as we are aware of them) to avoid getting pulled into the pit of failure's funk. The goal with any of these practices is for them to become useful and instinctual in our moment of need. The method we choose then becomes our go-to comfort in times of elevated alertness or a full-blown Emotional Hijack.

Ideally, what we want is to develop emotional agility. Emotional agility is a concept introduced by psychologist Susan David that refers to "being aware and accepting of all your emotions, even learning from the difficult ones. It also means getting beyond conditioned and preprogrammed cognitive and emotional responses (your hooks) to live in the moment with a clear reading of the present circumstances, respond appropriately, and then act in alignment with your deepest values."[4] Practicing the FREE model is a great way to build our emotional agility.

Liberators are a conscious response

Now that we've seen how our autopilot conspirator reactions (based on a threat or perceived threat) can be interrupted, what's next? Let's talk about how to engage and leverage our conscious brain in response to these threats. In exploring a new path, we can flip the script on our Conspirators, edit their weaknesses, and leverage their strengths, transforming them into Liberators that we can consciously choose.

The Liberators are specific actions we can implement that counteract the default Conspirators. This allows us to liberate ourselves from our autopilot failure response to begin learning and growing from failure. Depending on how we typically respond to failure (i.e. which Conspirator has a hold of us), these liberation actions may or may not seem all that different. However, unlike letting our Conspirators run the show, once we've reset or have interrupted an Emotional Hijack, all the Liberator's actions are available for us to *choose* instead of just reacting by default. We can try one or we can try them all. Experimenting with them all may open up a completely new way of seeing and experiencing the world around us. The best part is that now we have a way to course correct if things aren't going well. As Figure 18 depicts, we can unleash the Liberators.

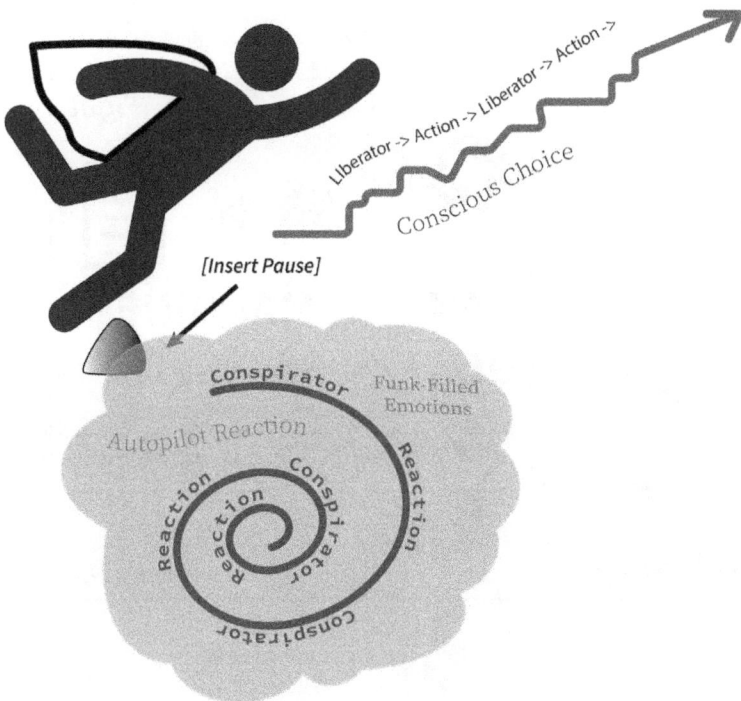

Figure 18   Unleash the Liberators

Figure 19 provides a visual of the Conspirator to Liberator flip. When we look at the strengths of the Machine, we see characteristics such as determination, focus, independence, and decisiveness. The Machine might be a good Liberator in an emergency where quick action needs to be taken or where deadlines are rapidly approaching. The Machine's perseverance can now serve us by switching from blindly plowing forward to focused diligence, executing to plan, and checking things off the list. By choosing the Machine Liberator, we are choosing the strategy of getting things done. We are charging ahead, decisive, and committed. The Machine's independent, determined nature can be of great service to us.

The Magician can also be a Liberator when harnessing its strengths such as optimism, agility, and seeing multiple sides of a situation. The Magician is especially adept at quickly assessing both the controllable and uncontrollable

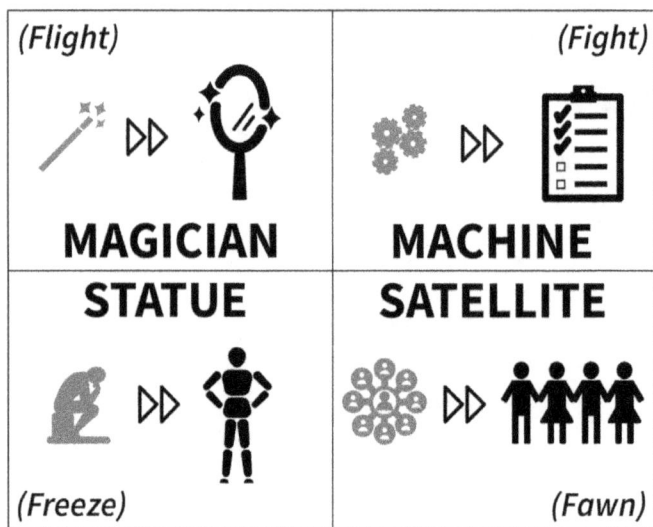

Figure 19   The Liberator matrix

factors in a failure allowing us to quickly change course in emergency situations where danger is beyond our control. When anticipating Tripping Hazards, the Magician Conspirator can see multiple factors that could trigger the failure thus providing time for mitigation strategies to be implemented to reduce or eliminate the impact altogether. When we harness the Magician persona's optimism we become like Teflon: nothing bad can stick to us and as a result we don't get stuck in situations that threaten our vitality. The Magician is also the spin doctor – painting a positive picture on negative outcomes, always looking for and finding the silver lining.

The Statue Liberator can be analytical and steadfast when not stuck in fear. When we harness the Statue persona's power, we remain calm amidst the chaos around us. The Statue asks many questions, not accepting the first option but holding steady until a broad range of options are reviewed. Much like a super-hero, the Liberated Statue embodies a power pose, refusing to crumble in the face of adversity. A good time to choose the Statue Liberator is in situations where thoughtful analysis is required so we don't jump to conclusions, especially where there may be significant consequences for our actions.

The Satellite Liberator can be adaptable, amiable in nature and thrive in community. As good coaches and managers know, leveraging the Satellite Liberator's innate ability to mediate and minimize conflict is critical to building trust and creating success. A good time to choose to be a Satellite would be in situations when leveraging the strength of the group would be most beneficial in giving us an added boost. Book clubs, professional societies, and even gyms often rely on the pull of the "team" to keep momentum moving in the right direction. When physical danger is present or in chaotic emergency situations there is often greater safety in numbers. Nothing like a mentor or teacher to help guide us when we are traveling new and unknown paths. (Hint: now would also be a great time to leverage the Satellite's connection by joining our community on Facebook: The Faceplant Book, if you haven't already.)

Inserting a pause allows us to flip from Conspirators to Liberators by removing active and passive control and avoidance and replacing them with conscious choice, as illustrated with our revised matrix below.

An interesting exercise we did during this book-writing journey was to examine our past failures selecting which Liberator we wish we'd chosen from our hindsight perspective. Here are a few examples.

- When it came to Melisa learning another language, she wishes that she'd chosen the Machine rather than Magician. She wants to be the person who hits the ground in a new country and immediately practices new words, Faceplants, and then tries again until she gets good enough to communicate; all the while laughing along with the native speakers at her missed pronunciation attempts.

- The rest of the story from Noël's Satellite Conspirator with her friend's mother comes after a particularly nasty interaction at a sleep-over where her friend was humiliated by her mother's behavior. Noël awoke the next morning determined that she was going to confront the mother about her alcoholism. In hindsight, she consciously chose the Machine Liberator after several years of operating from a Statue Conspirator. The confrontation didn't go well, but Noël knew she'd done the right thing. The mother did not acknowledge the impact until years later, but it was a necessary reality check for this woman to make changes in her life.

- It wasn't until beginning this work that Keeley realized the full impact the medical school exam had on her life. She could have chosen the Machine and just charged ahead, determined to study and not give up until she reached her goal. She could have chosen the Magician to see other options for coursework or alternate pathways to ultimately achieve the same outcome and leveraged the Magician's enduring optimism to reassure herself that things would eventually work out.

Identifying the Liberators we wish we had harnessed took actively digging into past experiences and the gift of many years' worth of hindsight. At this point in time, hindsight and wishing can't change the outcomes of our past failures. In order to consciously leverage these Liberators in the midst of an active Faceplant situation and *choose* our actions instead of reacting, we need to use the pause we talked about earlier to reality check our expectations.

Grounding expectations allows us to see clearly

Once we are in the "space," or have inserted a pause, we can then explore our expectations and see where a Tripping Hazard or Expectation Disconnect might be tripping us up. Our brains fill in the blanks of the story using a complex algorithm of past experiences, feelings, thoughts, etc., regardless of truth or context. Because of this, it's important to subject our stories to a truth filter. Asking the question "what do I know to be true?" repeatedly helps us filter out our Conspirators' fear-based stories and gets us back to the current reality. If our thoughts are saying "if I don't get this job, I'm a failure," we can ask what we know to be true about our

past job history and tell the story that "I know that I have gotten jobs in the past. Searching for jobs can be a difficult and
time-consuming process. My value does not decrease based
on someone else's inability to see my worth."

If our thoughts are saying "if I introduce myself to them,
they are going to laugh at me," we can ask what we know to
be true about previous social experiences and tell the story
that "I feel a little awkward when meeting new people. I have
successfully networked in the past. My current friends were
all once strangers too."

Fact-checking pointers

- **Hint 1**: Unless we are fortune tellers, anything we are
  telling ourselves about the future should immediately
  get the axe – we simply can't predict what will or won't
  happen in the future.
- **Hint 2**: Anything we are telling ourselves about someone else's actions should also get eliminated from our
  truth list – we cannot know 100% how people are
  going to react.
- **Hint 3**: Extremes are out. Things with "always, never,
  everyone, etc." are impossibilities due to the basic
  nature of the human experience. Remove them from
  the story.

Another important filter to help clarify our stories relates to
what we can control versus what we can't control. We try to
control others' perceptions by telling ourselves "one more
edit, one quick re-read, a little farther, a little faster... and
they'll see how great I am." Once again, we must remove the
false narrative that we can protect ourselves by controlling
other people's perceptions. Say it again, louder this time:
we can't control other people. When applying for a new job
we can control the story our application and resumes tell. We
can control what jobs we choose to apply for. We can control

advance preparation for an interview. We can control what we choose to wear and how we behave. We can't control how others perceive our fit for a role. We can't control the interview questions. We can't control the outcome. By understanding what we can control and letting go of the things we cannot, we open ourselves to an entirely different set of conscious actions instead of being stuck in fear and consumed by our autopilot conspirator's reactions.

Our conspirator mind also likes to dwell in binary (yes or no) solutions that are polarized opposites and all or nothing generalizations. "If I don't get this job, I am never going to get another job ever." "If this person doesn't call/text me back, I will be single forever." Rarely are any situations in life truly binary. Not only is there often a gray scale between black and white options, but often a vibrant rainbow of alternatives if only we pause and open our eyes long enough to see them. This is where *both/and* thinking can be leveraged to add space into our pause.[5] *Both/and* thinking takes out extremes and replaces them with options. It takes out "but" excuses and replaces them with "and" truths. It helps us change our perspective so that instead of seeing a door to a single room (a job, a person, a situation) being closed to us, we can see a hallway full of doors (multiple jobs, a world full of people, countless other situations), which remain open and may yield different results, better fits, and previously unimagined possibilities than the door that closed. An "if I don't get this job, I am never going to get another job" transforms into "if I don't get this job, it wasn't a good fit, and I got some new information that I can use to help find a better fit." An "if this person doesn't text/call, I will be single forever" turns into "if this person doesn't text or call, this personal interaction didn't work, and it illuminated several important factors I need to be aware of in future interactions." It is not about sugarcoating perceived failures, it is about grounding them in reality and understanding that in most situations, failures are not the end of the road, just a reason to check our compass and explore other paths.

As we go through life, we will be faced with many para-doxical situations (ones that seem to contradict themselves while also being interdependent). These situations are often seen as *either/or* situations. If we save all our money we may have financial security, but by not spending any money we may miss out on experiences and learning opportunities. Our mindset plays a critical role in how we approach these paradoxes. If we feel that we must choose, and only one choice is correct or right, we can find ourselves in a rut; for example, staying in a job that is comfortable but not fulfilling. We might overplay our strengths and avoid our weaknesses, which prevents us from learning, growing, and changing to meet the needs of the situation. These *either/or* scenarios force us into an autopilot response. We want to be able to short-circuit or interrupt an Emotional Hijack to minimize the time we spend deliberating with a decision.

Embracing paradoxes helps develop a growth mindset and naturally create *both/and* thinking. When examining assumptions, in the process of grounding expectations, there are three key areas to examine: knowledge (move from a sin-gle truth to multiple truths), resources (move from scarcity to abundance), and problem solving (move from controlling to learning). "Rather than assume the world is consistent, lin-ear and static, *both/and* thinking assumes the world is con-tradictory, circular and dynamic," write Professors Wendy K. Smith and Marianne W. Lewis.[6] In the next chapter, we'll talk more about developing a problem-solving mindset to facili-tate more *both/and* thinking options. For now, as we begin to ground our assumptions, we need to be honest with our-selves about what we know and what we really have available to work with.

Having expectations is part of being human. Problems arise when our expectations and reality aren't congruent. Learning to understand and manage our expectations through grounding or building a realistic picture allows us to achieve greater clarity. Examining our expectations regularly can act as a mental and emotional pressure relief valve. Now you may be thinking, ugh, how awful it is to have a section where we recommend embracing realism. Shouldn't we be dreamers? We aren't suggesting that you don't dream or have high expectations for yourself. However, by grounding our expectations, we open our eyes to one of the ways we get sucked into the gravity and disappointment of failure. Grounding expectations can be revealing and one of the most basic ways we can free ourselves from our own expectational drag.

We don't typically expect to fail and are therefore usually surprised when we Faceplant, even when we might have failed in the past. We don't actively seek out what doesn't work. We are looking for success, we are looking to win, and we automatically expect our efforts to be successful. We seldom consider failure as an option, which makes it difficult to anticipate it or learn from our failed efforts. Failures seem to be constantly springing out of our blind spots.

If only we could be more like the dragonfly. The dragonfly has two eyes consisting of 30,000 lenses and an additional three eyes with simple lenses. Amazingly, they have no blind spots. Grounding expectations can illuminate our potential blind spots by allowing us to be honest about our resources and helping us explore other options. We want to be more dragonfly-esque. With this increased visibility and self-awareness comes an acknowledgement and deeper understanding of our own thoughts and feelings. Owning these thoughts and feelings even when they are triggered by a failure, or "loss of face," will go a long way to creating a new perspective. In life there is so much that we can't control. However, by concentrating on what we can control, like our reactions to events and outcomes, we can begin to open our perspective and see the world through a broader filter.

The process of identifying things that might interfere with our plans should be complimented with effective ways to address these interferences. This preparation contingency planning has been shown to be very effective. Research

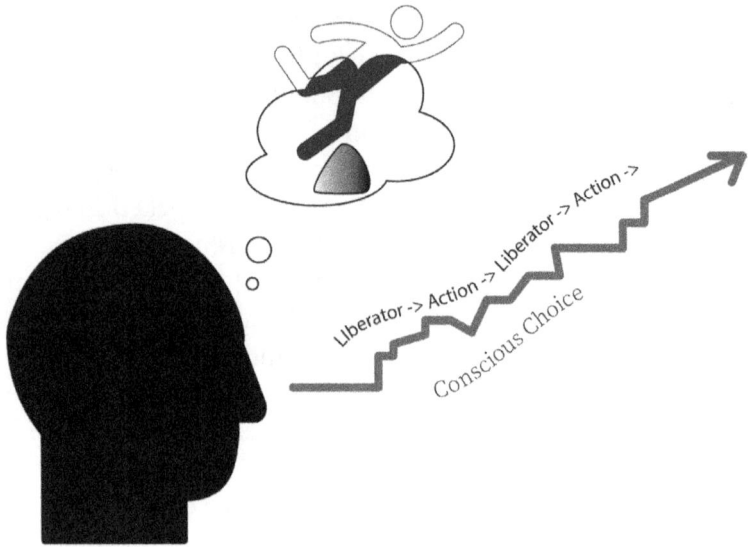

Figure 20   Anticipating tripping hazards

shows when we think through potential problems and identify possible solutions, the process helps us stay on track.
In essence we have identified potential obstacles that we
might encounter and created contingency plans for those
obstacles.[7]

When the three of us started reality checking our plans
for an upcoming event, we found that our expectations consistently exceeded what we were able to accomplish. Not only
that, but those expectations were incredibly out of whack
with what previous evidence would have indicated we could
do if we were paying attention. As a result, each week we
found ourselves frustrated and feeling like we'd failed, barely
keeping our heads above water. So much for freeing ourselves
from failure's funk. Sure, we could spot our Conspirators and
interrupt them, but we needed to do a better job of anticipating our Tripping Hazards if we really wanted to lift the gravity that was still threatening to sink us.

As described in the last chapter, we began with free form writing about the plans for the upcoming week and what we expected to accomplish or complete. It was only by realizing that our own expectations set us up to feel like we were consistently failing that we began to see how we could turn this around. Initially, we spent time at the beginning of the week listing expectations for the upcoming week. That simple act was almost comical in what it revealed. Noël's to-do list for a week had more on it than what could be completed in a month with no time allotted for sleep. Keeley's upcoming family road trip mental image was idyllic in the sights to be seen and memories to be made – a happy family visiting National Parks. The postcard image completely omitted the evidence that with four kids, two dogs and a huge RV, something was going to break, people were going to fight, important "things" would be forgotten, and GPS directions would try to kill them like had happened on EVERY OTHER TRIP EVER IN THE HISTORY OF THE HURLEY FAMILY.

After a few weeks of recognizing our nonsensical expectations, a template began to emerge that not only highlighted the disconnects with reality but also helped us prepare our Liberators for action when things did still go awry. We also included a place for reflection on the events of the previous week to take stock of what happened and to see how well we were able to call on our Liberators. When Noël realized the absurdity of her to-do list, she was able to create a new plan for the week that included chipping away at smaller chunks of her big projects while also prioritizing sleep and relationships. At the end of the week, she was absolutely gobsmacked at how much she was able to get done while feeling more rested than she had in years. Keeley went on her trip with clear eyes and plenty of evidence allowing her to laugh at the series of unfortunate events that would have previously sent her into hysterics. Forgotten socks (for a week of hiking!), a missing National Park Pass that had to be re-purchased, a broken door on the RV that randomly flew open while driving down the road, driving straight through a National Park without stopping because the spot the GPS told us to park was completely cordoned off, and a flat tire 30 minutes from the nearest town in the middle of the desert were only a few of the mishaps that had become giggle-able events instead of funk-filled freak-out sessions.

Again and again, we practiced this method, iterating and tweaking as we went, and we were constantly amazed at the efficacy of this simple exercise. The Anticipated Events exercise we developed minimizes our blind spots, allowing us to see more of what's possible. We created a form that is included in the Toolbox at the end of this book to share what worked for us, but don't feel locked into what we did. Create one or modify ours, it doesn't need to be formal, it just needs to help you see where your expectations might be askew so they can be adjusted appropriately. The Anticipated Events method we developed helped us prepare for potential Faceplants by looking at upcoming events and our expectations around them (Hello, Tripping Hazards!). The following are a list of questions we found to be helpful in the Anticipated Events exercise and Noël has included an example in Toolbox 3.

Anticipated Events worksheet questions

- Goal/Situation/Event: Describe the facts.
- What do you expect to happen? What thoughts are you having?
- Describe what you want to have happen regarding this goal/situation/event.
- What might trigger an Emotional Hijack, a Conspirator?
- In the case of a trigger and Emotional Hijack, how will you handle it?
- Which Liberator could you leverage instead?
- What would be a realistic expectation?
- What preparation/mitigation actions might you take? What cautions, warning signs, or red flags might exist?

- What signs will indicate that a Conspirator is appearing?
- What preparation/mitigation actions might you take if your Conspirator appears?
- What was the outcome?

The interesting part of this exercise is that we found, with time, we were able to interrupt our Conspirators just by looking at our expectations and reality checking our stories. We often greatly overestimate what we can accomplish and drastically underestimate how much time things will take, so by just acknowledging the ridiculousness of our expectations, we reduced the stress we inflicted on ourselves and interrupted our Conspirators before they even had the chance to hijack us.

Grounding expectations isn't about silencing our voices, limiting our view, or suppressing emotions or thoughts. We can still express ourselves fully and have great expectations for ourselves. By seeing problems from multiple perspectives like a dragonfly, we can begin to use our increased awareness to explore our contribution to our failures and/or systemic contributions that have nothing to do with us. This exercise forces us to be honest with ourselves, about our actions that contribute to failure. When we are looking from a constructive filter, aware of our own expectations, then we can begin to look for productive solutions in the future.

Pre-mortems can help us be better prepared

In the Reflect chapter, we used several tools to identify areas of improvement or uncover systemic issues for change. These are all tools we can use to examine event lessons after they occur so we can learn, and they are incredibly useful for examining the outcome of our actions. The Anticipated Events exercise allows us to learn through hypothetical hindsight. There are so many benefits to this method, not just the benefit of identifying prospective problems.

There is another fantastic tool that harnesses these benefits by aiding in anticipating possible failure outcomes, sensitizing ourselves to the signs of trouble, and creating the most likely chance of success. That tool is the Pre-mortem.

Hold. The. Phone. Isn't preparing for failure all but guaranteeing that failure will occur? Not exactly. It's about creating if/then scenarios: "If" this thing happens, "then" I will do this. It's about looking at what could happen to trip us up and planning for how we will respond if it does so that we're not as easily hijacked by our Conspirators jumping up and carrying us away. The Pre-mortem gives us the structure in which our if/then scenarios can be successfully vetted.

In a Pre-mortem, we imagine a time at some point in the future and pretend that whatever endeavor we are currently about to take on has already happened and has already ended in failure. From that futuristic vantage point, we then look back and brainstorm about what factors or events could have come into play to cause us to fail. It's like a time machine forward with a reverse crystal ball, or something like that. Pre-mortems are great for big projects, but we've also found them to be especially helpful in our day-to-day life. The steps to a Pre-mortem are: 1) Brainstorm what could have caused the failure, 2) Identify red flags that might indicate one of those failure causes is coming, 3) Identify mitigations that can be put in place to prevent those failures from happening and/or actions that will be taken if a red flag or failure appears, and 4) Identify the time frame those mitigations have to be in place for there to be a successful outcome of the activity. Lost? We've included an example in Toolbox 2.

We naturally expect our new ventures or efforts to be successful. We tend toward confirmation bias where we only consider the evidence that supports our being successful in whatever we are undertaking. Our expectation is that our efforts will be successful. Failure isn't considered. It's not on our radar as we launch something new and exciting, and this makes it more difficult to learn from our failed efforts.

In this Pre-mortem exercise, we have fast forwarded through the initial excitement and optimism to a pretend future where this project has already been completed and failed miserably. We then work backward to determine all the ways that our endeavor failed. We aren't looking for what might go wrong. We are assuming failure and asking what did go wrong that resulted in the failure. We want to capture all the reasons for this failure. Voilà! Now we have the list of everything we need to watch out for as we embark on the project, job, or venture. This exercise substantially increases the chances of success.[8]

The unexpected happens

If you're thinking "that's great and all, but what about all that stuff that we can't predict and don't see coming? How the heck are we supposed to interrupt our Conspirators during a sneak attack??!!" No matter how prepared we are by grounding our expectations and creating a Pre-mortem, we cannot anticipate everything. There are still events that come at us from left field. At some point in all our lives, there will be unexpected events that completely derail us. We will have many unanticipated happy surprises as well as sad or stressful events. These might include trials like a cancer diagnosis, sudden death, request for divorce or breakup, or loss of a job. Failures, traumas, and other life-altering events can catch us off our guard, completely unaware.

This is exactly why we did all the work in the *Focus*, *Reflect*, and *Explore* stages, so that when unpredictable surprise scenarios pop up, we already know our Usual Suspect, can see and feel the red flags in our bodies, and can leverage a Liberator to get out of our fear-based reactions and into conscious action. It's certainly not easy and doesn't always go according to plan, but it can work, and we were completely surprised by how well it usually worked when it did. The following story by Keeley illustrates the sneak attack nature of these surprise situations and their equally surprising outcome when we can fight tooth and nail to fend off our Conspirators and harness a Liberator instead.

Keeley's story

It's 6:30 am on a Thursday. I remind my daughter, Emmy, of her rapidly approaching retainer check. Rushing around, loading the car, we take off right at 7 am. The GPS says we can make it on time. Ten minutes into the trip and I tell her to get her retainers in. She can't find them. Are you kidding me right now?!?! RED FLAG RED FLAG RED FLAG!!! Off roading on the shoulder to spin the car around and head towards home. After multiple calls home, no one can find the retainer.

The retainer is nowhere to be found, and we are 30 minutes late. The nurse informs me it will be $400+ dollars to replace them. My head explodes. I try to breathe. This makes no sense. She lost one on the bottom before and it was no charge.

Orthodontist Staff: We only replace them once.
Conspirator-me thinks: Just pay the money and move on.
[PAUSE]
Liberator me asks: What are our other options?
Staff: Um, we can call the doctor and see what we can do?
Me: OK, thank you.
[Emmy and I exit office in silence. Driving home in silence, the phone rings.]
Staff: We got in contact with doctor, he understands your frustration.
[They proceed to explain how we'll work it out.]
Me: Yes, we can do that, thank you for working with the doctor to resolve this. [HANG UP]

Emmy and I exchange a glance of disbelief. We can't believe that worked. We grab breakfast. We get new retainers made. I do not pay the replacement fee. I drop her off at school and head to work at 11 am (but what I really want is a beer and a nap, that was exhausting).

Reflection: I am almost always a Statue or Satellite when it comes to confrontation – just take my money and I will think of all the things I should have said later… for weeks and weeks… berating myself all the while. Choosing the Machine was a mind-blowing experience that worked out far better than I could have imagined. This was HUGE for me and was verifiable evidence (in stark contrast to the incessant story in my head) that tries to convince me that conflict always ends poorly and should be avoided at all costs.

The learning curve is helpful on this journey

In addition to calling on our Liberators when our spidey senses detect fear, we can also leverage the learning curve we discussed in Part 1. By being honest with ourselves on where we fall on the learning curve regarding a particular subject or situation, we can realign our expectations to where we are in the process. Normalizing the negative feelings we feel as we start the downward slope portion of "knowing what we don't know and it's a lot" can help us see what we need to do to keep moving forward and work toward the upward trajectory portion of the curve. It can also help us to make a conscious decision on whether to continue pushing forward or not. Sometimes pushing through will cause us more harm than good. Sometimes pushing through will send us barreling at full speed with our eyes closed into a brick wall. Opening our eyes, getting our bearings on the curve, and understanding the path that lies ahead are key to making an informed decision on whether to proceed or not. If we do choose to

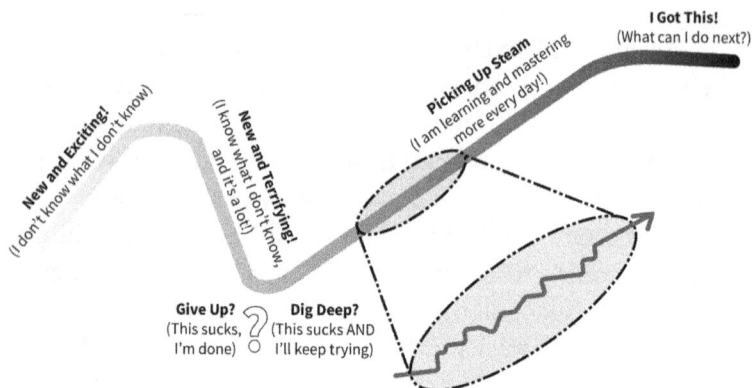

Figure 21   The learning curve magnified

proceed, we can do so with the realistic expectation that the upward slope of learning will not be flat, as Figure 21 shows, but full of its own peaks, valleys, and setbacks.

We can also embrace a beginner's mindset to help mitigate some of our Expectation Disconnects. When children learn to walk, we don't expect them to stand up, look us in the eye, and sashay across the floor. We expect them to struggle with balance, fall, find props to help them get upright, fall again, lurch, lean, and contort their way to a tiny forward motion, fall more (sometimes hilariously, sometimes terrifyingly), and repeat the process again and again over weeks and months until they reach the confidence and ability of a drunken sailor – hooray! At some point in our journey to adulting, we lose this expectation of trial and error and replace it with "I need to protect my curated image and can't show weakness in the form of failure" and/or "I should be good at this" straight out of the gate. Anything that shows evidence against the "I am good at this" mentality is met with a shovel to bury it where no one can see it, get away from it as quickly as possible, or avoid it at all costs. "I'm not good at foreign languages," gives us permission to not try, to avoid looking foolish for mispronouncing something, to avoid embarrassment when we use the wrong word, to deflect attacks on our sense of intelligence. Learning languages (or any new skill for that matter) is HARD, complex, nuanced, and often confusing. By embracing a beginner's mindset, we acknowledge all of that *and* we do it anyway. We cheer on small victories, we treat failures as key data points, *and* we keep checking our expectations to make sure we are seeing the struggle as critical to the process. We keep exploring our options, each time reminding ourselves that we are a perpetual beginner.

Some of the tools we have shared may resonate with you and some may not. Some may work in some situations, some may not work at all. Some may get amazing results, others not so much. Exploring different tools and methods for identifying our Tripping Hazards, identifying red flags that warn us about our Conspirators, and unleashing our Liberators to choose a different course of action is an ongoing process that evolves over time. But if we can make this wild experiment work, we're 100% confident you can too.

TL;DR

- Liberators are our chosen conscious responses to Emotional Hijacks. Liberators are the exact opposite of our Conspirators, who operate in autopilot. Liberators set us free from these conspiracy paths and help us learn and grow.
- Redefining what failure means in our own lives gives us freedom from the past. Ideally, failure will be a welcome teacher, but it will take time and practice to get to that point.
- Learning how to interrupt an emotional fire alarm is a first step toward freedom. Four methods are presented that can interrupt or help reduce the recovery time from an Emotional Hijack: meditation, mindfulness, pause and breathe, and a physical cue.
- The Anticipated Events exercise allows us to see clearly and opens up additional possibilities. We

can learn to guide emotions to gain greater access to response options using filters like "what I can control/can't control," etc.

- Anticipating potential Tripping Hazards can help us avoid an Emotional Hijack.
- Pre-mortems can help us be better prepared to address failure risks.
- Unexpected events will continue to happen. Practicing before an event with the Emotional Hijack interruption methods will create increased awareness.

Where the rubber hits the road

Grab your journal.

- Consider situations in your own life where failure tends to trip you up.
  1. When might the Machine's "stand and fight" response be a good Liberator to choose?
  2. Under which circumstances might the Magician's flee, either literally or figuratively, be a good option?
  3. When might it be a good option to stop and think like the Statue Liberator rather than act immediately?
  4. When would keeping the peace or compromising your own will be a good option like the Satellite Liberator?
- Try writing down your old definition of failure. Create a new definition that will serve you in what you want for your life.
- Try the Anticipated Events exercise in the Toolbox. Look at your upcoming week and then check back afterwards to close the loop on the exercise.
- Read through the Pre-mortem example in the Toolbox. Take an upcoming project or event and go through the exercise.

Chapter 7

Engage in flipping the script

"Sometimes, I crash and burn. Always, I crash and learn," writes Kari Byron.

A fun way to engage in life is through experimentation. You may not be a scientist or an engineer and that's OK. Melisa and Keeley both have science/engineering backgrounds, Noël doesn't. (Before you get too nervous, this material is completely Noël approved. She has kept the two of us from geeking out over the top.) The engagement journey (aka, life with all our successes and failures) is unique for each of us humans. Taking on life through experimentation can look a lot of different ways. Whether you are a natural experimenter or a first timer, this chapter is about how to engage with life in a new way. It is about living life with a fiercely curious mindset each day, about rethinking assumptions, testing them out, and engaging in a myriad of options. It's about just running the experiment and engaging with life as if you were a scientist discovering your own journey.

The journey is the process we go through in life; in other words, it's all the steps we take along the path that gets us to a new skill or next level of knowledge. As opposed to solely concentrating on the goal or outcome of our experiments or of our lives, let's put our attention on the quality of our journey. This approach to life, both successes and failures, can help us learn and grow stronger independent of the outcome (failure, rejection, defeat, tie, or success). Why is this important?

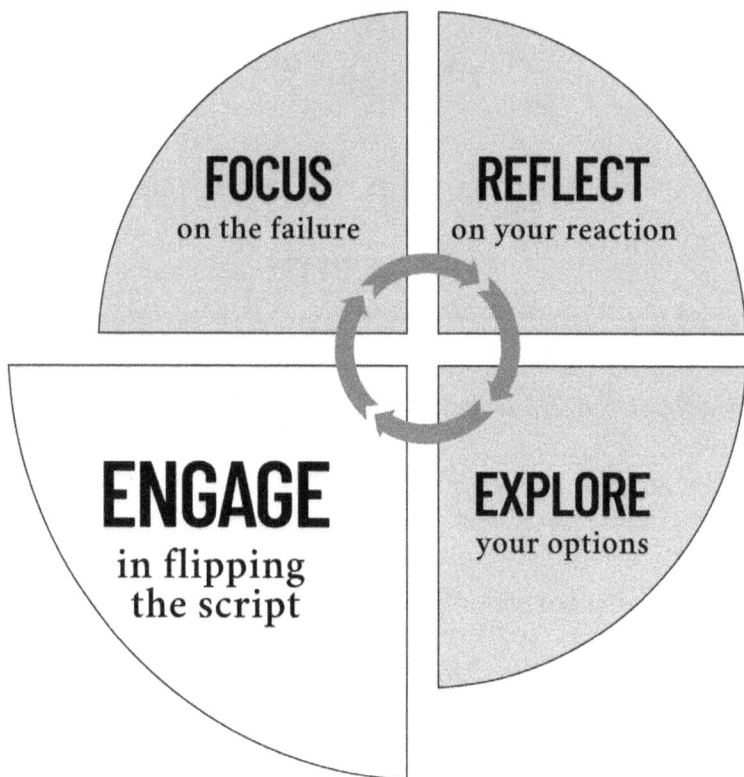

Figure 22   Engage in flipping the script

Failure is going to happen whether we plan for it or not. (Obvious, we know.) However, as we've already discussed, failure isn't something we expect or anticipate when we try something new or different. Recall, in the new definition of failure, failure is our *sensei*, our teacher. It is by failing that we discover the formula for success. Failure is as important to success as water is to fish. How can we make failure our fuel? Let's jump in.

Problem solving can be cool!

We know it may sound nerdy but problem solving is one of the best mindsets/approaches to bring to our lives. A problem solver is someone who embraces problems as they occur or sees them merely as an opportunity for improvement. They are curious and resourceful in examining why something happened. A problem solver looks for the true, real cause of the problem; what engineers call the root, the underlying or fundamental cause of the problem. A problem solver then evaluates all possible solutions – those that only contain the problem and those that address the root cause. After we do this a few times, our confidence grows, and we begin to naturally approach problems from this perspective. One of our favorite nerds on television was the co-host of the popular show, *MythBusters*, Kari Byron. In case you're not familiar with Byron or the show, let's talk about her approach to starring on a television show about experimentation.

Kari Byron grew up hating science class. She hated all the memorization. She wanted to be inspired and have her curiosity peaked. Byron wasn't a scientist in any sense of the word. However, she grew into a science expert because of her approach to problem solving. She fell in love with science and experimentation. She got to don a lab coat and be a science nerd. She didn't need to have a PhD or even an engineering degree to be on *MythBusters*. She just needed to be fiercely curious. She wondered what would happen and then tested theories. Her experiments were simple: from putting Mentos in a Coke bottle to running a bull through a china shop. She describes her style of experimentation as being more like "crash testing." She and the *MythBusters'* team were just having fun, solving problems, and figuring out how things worked. Regarding her time on the show, Byron writes: "We employed the scientific method, the perfect narrative vehicle for proving and disproving myths."[1]

Let's talk about using the scientific method for problem solving. The scientific method is a systematic, organized process for arranging thoughts, facts, and ideas, which lends itself to confirmation by experimentation. We can think of problem solving like our FREE wheel. A wheel is circular and is intended to keep rolling and going forward. A wheel

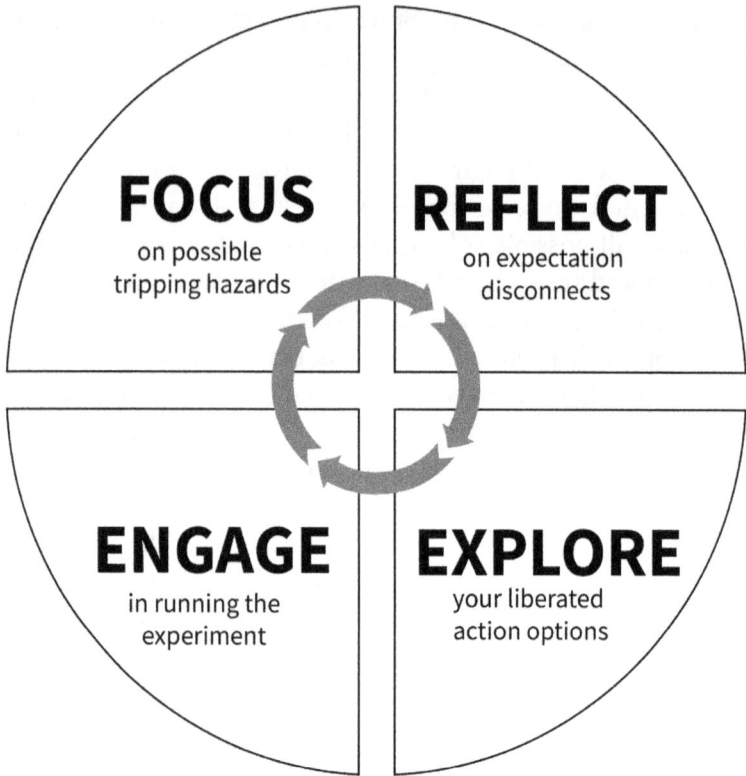

Figure 23   The FREE Method Revisited

isn't designed to just roll once. That's the approach we'd like to propose with problem solving and experimentation. Our wheel consists of four quadrants showing the FREE model cycle.[2] Reflection is an essential step in the problem-solving action of getting to the underlying cause. If we understand the fundamental cause of success and failure, we will better understand our next steps. We can use this knowledge as a guide.

1. The *Focus* step is our fact-checking phase; this is where we ask all kinds of questions and dig deep into understanding the underlying problem. We should question what we know, have heard, or think we

know. We strive to maintain an objective observer perspective where outcomes are neither deemed good nor bad – they are simply more data to analyze and learn from.

2. The *Reflect* step is arguably the most important phase because of the synthesis of information. In this step, we examine the outcomes of previous experiments and what we expect to happen in subsequent trials. Reflection can take the form of studying by first analyzing what happened, then looking at why it happened, and finally working to understand the mechanisms at play. We can question what worked or didn't work in the past and why it worked or didn't work.

3. *Explore* is where we begin to investigate our options. We want to look at the current situation and decide what success would look like and create a theory about how to get there. We identify our assumptions, hypotheses, and theories and how we might test both the obvious and the complex. We are in essence planning our experiment. What do we want to try? What might happen if we try one solution versus another solution? The Anticipated Events exercise can be helpful here. During the *Explore* step, we decide what we are going to try next.

4. In the Engage step we run the experiment(s) and collect data on what happened. We test our assumptions, hypotheses, and theories. Engagement is the time for digging into the analysis; this is where we identify adjustments and decide on the next experiments or create an update. If the results are moving us closer to our desired state, then we can incorporate these methods into the way we do things. If we've achieved our goal, we may choose to stop. If the results still aren't our desired end state, then we may want to adjust our assumptions, flush out new options that have revealed themselves through our experimentation, and start the cycle again.

There are times when experimental results are inconclusive or the factors are confounded (interact with one another). In this case, it's important to acknowledge what is true before taking next steps. (This leads to a whole other level of experimentation – which Melisa is happy to completely geek out about.)

On the television show, Byron goes about flinging herself into experimentation and paying attention to the results. She describes gaining wisdom by asking the questions rather than knowing the answers. She increased her knowledge and experience with each myth she tested. Byron wrote: "To be successful, you don't need to be right, but you do have to understand, with a scientist's emotional detachment, why you were wrong."[3] To truly learn from our failures, we must develop strong reflection muscles.

As a scientist, Melisa has experimented her whole life both inside and outside of work. She once did an experiment to drive a different way to work each day for 30 days. She has had cooking successes and massive disasters from experimentation (think loaves of bread that could be used for bricks or loaves that were perfect on the exterior and still raw dough in the center). She's also conducted hundreds of experiments inside the lab optimizing processes used to make computer chips. She does it because she loves discovering something new. Melisa isn't afraid to just jump in and do something new or different. Well, in certain areas of life, that is. In the story below, she shares her mindset around experimentation.

Melisa's story

Experimentation for me is about discovery. I fell in love with experimentation during my graduate work and continued to experiment over the years in my different career roles. I discovered that I could fail in 90% or even 100% of my experiments. However, because I was able to use the information from the failed runs to improve the next experiment, all was not lost.

Over time, I realized that I wanted to take my love of experimentation beyond my career to other areas of my life and share my findings with others. I started experimenting with where I wanted to live, leadership roles in various organizations, real estate investing, genealogy, learning to speak French, and writing – just to name a few. Some experiments have been successful, and others have failed. And, yes, I am still deathly afraid to attempt speaking French in front of another person.

Let me tell you about how I've engaged in a few experiments with regard to my writing.

Writing this book is one example of my experimentation. It took me five years to write my first book, *Problem Solving for New Engineers*. I didn't want this book to take quite so long. Experiment! Write a book with colleagues… would it be faster? The answer is yes but not by much. I started writing on my own for roughly a year, then I approached Noël and Keeley. I knew that I had something to say about failure, but thought collaborating in dialogue and writing with others might help clarify concepts and ideas and produce a better product. That's how this book began.

During the crunch time, as our first book draft deadline quickly approached, I played with the length of time I sat down to write. After a few trials, I reached the conclusion that 30 minutes of intense work followed by taking a break to walk around, do laundry, read a book, or make lunch felt more productive.

I've also experimented with my daily writing habit. I noticed that I would wake up and have a million things on my mind. I started setting a timer for 10 minutes and writing down everything I was thinking of – just to clear my head. I did this first thing in the morning or in the middle of the night, and I experienced feeling calmer. Writing for 10 minutes for the purpose of clearing my head has now become a daily practice.

Now, after all these years of experimenting with writing, I don't mind writing crap when I know I've got a good idea. I have plenty of evidence to show that the writing process works to bring focus to those ideas. There are times when I need to write a paragraph of nothings just to get started. Getting started is still the hardest part. That will be my next experiment!

As you can see from Melisa's story, she has a unique mind-set when it comes to experimentation. Let's talk more about mindset before leaving the problem-solving topic. Armed with our new definition of failure as our master teacher and our growth mindset, failure offers us opportunity. Growth and learning come from failure, from struggle, stretching, and adversity. A growth mindset will use failures to get better and better, maximizing potential. By pivoting away from a setback, failure, or mistake, we can focus our attention on what there is to learn; we can see each of these failures as steppingstones on our journey. Think of the failure, the mistake, or error simply as information. The information we gain tells us what didn't work. We may call it a failure, but with our new definition, what we are really saying is "that trial didn't work, but I'm a problem solver. I'll just try something else."

Embracing our natural curiosity opens new possibilities for life

We were born naturally curious. When we were children, we asked a million questions annoying our parents to no end. We wanted to know everything about the world around us.

Over time, that curiosity was discouraged. From the cautionary tale of Curious George, the fictional little monkey whose curiosity leads him into all sorts of trouble to the repeated frustrated responses from our parents of "because I said so" in response to our incessant inquiries, we learned that curiosity was not appreciated and valued.[4] Our early childhood "whys" and "why nots" were replaced with a tacit acceptance of "this is just the way things are."

The problem with this negative attitude toward curiosity is that curiosity is an essential ingredient in progress. Curiosity is required for invention, development, learning, and growth. Curiosity is required for effective problem solving.[5]

What if we all amped up our curiosity and became infinitely curious about our precious lives? When we were living in autopilot mode, we couldn't afford to be curious. We were so concerned about surviving the perceived threat, we couldn't even stop and consider our actions. With curiosity we can explore how to live fully intentional lives where growth is an expectation. We can't live on autopilot *and* be intentional with the way we live our lives. Intentionality means that our habits are aligned with our values. Dave declared his commitment to losing weight. He tried for several weeks, then realized that he was more committed to eating anything he wanted, anytime he wanted to eat it, than he was to losing weight. Wanting something and being committed to something are very different things. When we commit to something new, it requires that we create new habits. "A mind that is open to growth and change is a hub from which values and goals can be brought to life and realized. There is tremendous empowerment in appointing yourself the agent of your life – in taking ownership of your own development, career, creative spirit, work and connections," write Professors Wendy K. Smith and Marianne W. Lewis in *Both/And Thinking*. Our mindset and commitment are required to deliver the intentionality necessary for growth. Smith and Lewis continue: "It's about bringing a playful sense of curiosity, experimentation, and what ifs to bear in the service of living."[6]

Most of our basic assumptions and beliefs about life were formed years and years ago. Is something that we experienced or believed at 9 still true at 19, 39, or 59? Let's begin with the premise that at any age, we all have theories, models, principles, etc., about how the world around us works. These theories may be based on our educational training or experiences but for most people, our theories, models, principles, etc., are not built from formal education. Our model of the world is built from our experiences as human beings, and it's somewhat random based on what we saw as we developed into the person we are today.[7] One way to think of learning is simply updating these theories, models, principles, etc., based on new information that we gather from our experiences. Learning helps us understand why things work or don't, why things happen or don't, and why some decisions work and some don't. When we are successful, we have learned what to do. We can often repeat this and be successful again. When we fail, we have learned what not to do. However, we still don't know what to do to be successful. In failure, we are eliminating what doesn't work. We've eliminated one possible solution. Therefore, the correct solution must be one of the other possible choices, one that hasn't been proven wrong yet. Even trying to explain this is confusing. This way of thinking can create a cognitive barrier, which requires the need for some mental gymnastics and curiosity if we are to learn from our failures. Looking at it another way, the first time we try something we are starting with no experience. When we begin again after failure, we are beginning with an experience of what didn't work. While it may feel like we are back at ground zero, we have added to our foundational knowledge and elevated our vantage point. Embracing our curious nature then allows us to see additional options in our effort to figure out what might work.

Curiosity can help us adopt the perspective that our mistakes and failures are simply things that didn't work. If we screw up, we don't have to start over; we can begin where we are. For example, if we commit to skip dessert for a week but one night we forget, we don't have to restart the experiment or give up. Reflect on the conditions that led to forgetting and then experiment with changing those conditions. Make failure fuel for change. When your best friends come over with brownies to watch a movie, discovering that grabbing one is a habit can be a great spark to try a new experiment. (BTW, Noël is famous for her brownies at gatherings.) The experiment may be to match those brownies with healthier alternatives or maybe ask your friend to bring an alternate dessert that you don't like. But what if we make the same mistake repeatedly? In this case, we aren't learning from mistakes or failures. We are deciding, like Dave earlier, that our commitment to the status quo is more important than growing in this area of our lives.

We can reframe everything we are curious about or want to try as an experiment or draft. This framing ensures that we don't expect perfection. Curiosity can even help us examine our regrets without judgment. If we can leverage curiosity with our regrets, we can eliminate the "if only" pontification that poses unobtainable hypothetical outcomes and instead asks us to choose the "at least" ending to examine what we learned. With curiosity "if only I had passed the MCAT, I would have become a world-renowned epidemiologist" becomes "at least I discovered the limitless medical treatments lasers provide to help more people than I could have imagined." We can replace the funk of failure that sabotages our self-confidence and demotivates us with curiosity that inspires us.

Limit the blast zone for failures

Along with our curiosity, we can create opportunities to fail on a small scale. Well thought out experiments are a great way to make this happen. If we intentionally experiment with small experiments (James Clear's *Atomic Habits*) so that we can fail in small ways, we limit the effected zone from those failures.[8] There's no need to jump into something that will result in a massive failure. We can set our goals a little higher than we think we can reach (just outside our comfort zone). We can try to make each decision point an experiment. We can test out small assumptions. If something proves false or fails, we can unlearn it quickly. As a result, we know more than we did before, and we have useful information about the problem we're trying to solve. Creating a culture of experimentation in our lives allows us to see failure as an opportunity to test our theories, challenge beliefs, and adjust as needed. The idea of finding patterns/building models in everything we do while maintaining that "life-is-an-experiment" mentality (scientific thinking) is a great way to explore life.

We must jump into the unknown with experimentation. Even failures generate new information that we didn't have before the experiment. Regardless of the outcome, through the process of experimentation, we learn more than we knew before. The more we can embrace this view of failure, the better off we will be. Let's bring curiosity and playfulness into our lives. We don't need test tubes or computers, just an open and curious mind. As we begin experimenting, we need to make the experiments personal. This allows us to be responsible for our own growth and learning.

Experiment with your Conspirators

Experimenting with our own Conspirators is a great way to begin. Here's a simple three-step way to get started:

1. Identify the area of life where you'd like to improve.
2. List ideas for testing different ways of responding. Feel free to crowdsource ideas with friends, family, colleagues, or mentors.
3. Write down what success would look like.

One great suggestion from business strategist and author Greg McKeown is to put bounds on our experiments.[9] Because there's a certain momentum or inertia required to make course corrections, setting bounded ranges up front, much like guard rails, can create some ease around making decisions and adjustments if a course correction is needed. The upper bound should be set high enough to represent substantial progress but not so high that we become burned out trying to achieve it. The lower bound should be high enough to keep us inspired but not so low that we achieve it even with unexpected interruptions or minimal effort. The bounded range may look something like "never less than x, but more than y." For Melisa the bounded range for writing is never less than writing a paragraph a day but never more than a chapter a day.

If we experiment with applying bounded ranges to the Machine Conspirator, where accomplishing is a driving focus, the right bounded range can lead to a rhythm of accomplishment and reprieve that flows in an almost effortless fashion. The Machine might also want to experiment with quitting or altering course. Persistence is not about staying on a path no matter what. Persistence is about finding the right path to reach your goal (and there may be several paths). Sticking to a bad decision, a bad path or direction doesn't demonstrate commitment and sound decision making. Learning when to quit and when to grit is critical for learning and growing. Quitting should be viewed as a decision-making tool. The sooner we can start making course corrections the sooner we get on the right path. The Machine must be able to both quit or grit depending on the changing circumstances of a situation.

The Magician in experimental mode might try a tool like the magic mirror. Much like the wicked stepmother when she discovered that she wasn't the fairest in the land, our own magic mirror can be a brutal fact-teller that strips away our excuse-laden armor and gets straight to the truth.

If the Magician previously said, "I was late because of traffic," the magic mirror says, "No, you were late because you didn't estimate the travel time properly, you didn't check the GPS, and you didn't prioritize adding a buffer to your arrival time." By acknowledging the honest role we play in both successes and failures, we can free ourselves from the helplessness of our self-induced victimization and regain our power to choose differently going forward. The Pre-mortem or the Anticipated Events exercises are great tools for analyzing upcoming events because the Magician has the ability to uncover the array of factors that could trip them up. It might even be beneficial to go through the FREE method exercises with some successes to examine our role in what really happened, thus ensuring Tripping Hazards aren't lurking in the shadows ready to induce a Faceplant the next time we do the same activity.

The Statue can experiment with asking questions and taking small experimental steps to test the waters in a new space. One test might include finding a safe space and experimenting with blurting out gut feelings. The Statue would benefit from trying expansive *both/and* thinking to find and run an experiment that includes options from both sides of their proverbial fence.[10]

The Satellite may practice disagreeing with the group and suggesting other options. In a kind way, the Satellite can explain their point of view first and listen for others' response. Additionally, the Satellite could be the first in their circle to try something new, whether a restaurant or a new venue, to experiment with forging the path for self and friends.

Practice helps strengthen our learning muscles

As we discussed earlier in the book, one of the key ways we learn new skills is through practice. Practice is more than repetition. Practice is the struggle to overcome failures repeatedly. For someone to exhibit a skill masterfully, they have had to work hard, struggle, and practice a lot. It is through practice that our brain begins to change. Practice is a necessary and essential part of performing well. Taking small steps and getting immediate feedback are good beginnings. This allows for smaller, learning-sized mistakes without jumping whole hog into the fear zone.

Recall that to begin learning, we need to stretch outside of where we are comfortable. To learn and grow, we must want to push outside our comfort zone into the learning zone. We will need to dwell in the discomfort of doing something new long enough for us to grow, however long that takes. Growth happens in the learning zone where we are struggling. We learn when we stretch, practice, engage with challenging experiences, and spend time in reflection. We need to stay in the learning zone long enough for the new skill to create a new connection and myelination to begin.

After enough practice and struggle, we are eventually back into our comfort zone. However, after a new skill has been added to our quiver, our comfort zone is enlarged and expanded. Our goal is to achieve a level of competency where we feel comfortable performing the new skill. Before we achieve that competency, however, it takes courage to push ourselves into that learning zone to begin the learning process. We are likely to even experience some fear in the learning zone but with a problem-solving mindset, we can choose not to let the fear stop us. Struggle, in the learning zone, is an uncomfortable place to find ourselves. However, by remaining in the learning zone and working through the struggle, we have the opportunity to learn.[11]

If this is all sounding like déjà vu, we know, we did this on purpose because it's super important. When we're struggling and uncomfortable, it's easy to slip back into the funk, to let our expectations get out of whack and get hijacked by Conspirators. Reminding ourselves of how we learn and the effort and experimentation that is required for growth can help us reality check our expectations and call our Liberators back in to help.

Aside from remembering how we learn, an important part of the reality check during this practicing phase is to develop a realistic assessment of our strengths and weaknesses. If we believe we are smarter, stronger, or more skilled than we are, we can become complacent or impatient. If on the other hand, we feel we are worse off than we think, we can feel defeated and throw in the towel without giving ourselves a fair chance. This accurate self-assessment is the foundation for improvement. When we completely understand where our strengths and weaknesses lie, we can target our practices accordingly. This work is the grit, determination, and persistence required for personal growth to take place.

Recall that new skills are developed through creation of new neural circuitry and strengthening the myelin sheath surrounding the nerve fibers. The myelin sheath both facilitates the signal communication and strengthens it, growing thicker the more we practice.

Myelin is also strengthened by slowing down because the more we slow down our practice the more closely we can monitor and correct mistakes, leading to increased precision and understanding.[12] By reflecting on our mistakes, we learn to observe, judge, and strategize our own performance. With reflection we develop strategies that allow us to fix things. There's no blame or shame. Experts have "developed something more important than mere skill." They have "grown a detailed conceptual understanding that allows them to control and adapt their performance, to fix problems, and to customize their circuits to new situations."[13]

With this additional knowledge of myelin, our attitude toward failure can be different. With every subsequent practice or experiment, we can allow ourselves to linger in the discomfort a little longer each time. This provides an opportunity for us to reflect on our feelings, thoughts, and opinions about the failure. Failure doesn't have to be a setback or the writing on the wall that we don't have a future in this skill. Failures are key steppingstones on the path to that new skill and a new future! This is not necessarily an easy journey. Not only is struggle hard, it takes courage and a lot of self-compassion to face our Conspirators head on. The psychologist Abraham Maslow wrote: "One can choose to go back toward safety or forward toward growth. Growth must be chosen again and again; fear must be overcome again and again."[14] Sadly, this isn't a one-and-done exercise!

Continuous improvement is a lifelong journey

As we've just read, growth isn't a one-time, done-and-dusted deal. We must choose it over and over. Each time we allow ourselves to be vulnerable by leaving our comfort zone, we must be deliberate and intentional. It may get easier with time, but that doesn't mean it's easy. Implied in this approach is acknowledging that while we may not be where we want to be, we can still get there – we just aren't there *yet*. There is something more to learn and another area where we can grow. We can always get better, even if it feels like we are just getting better at failing. Becoming a lifelong learner requires persistent reflection and small continual improvements – focus on the baby steps.

In the spirit of lifelong learning and continuous improvement, we want to introduce a few more Japanese concepts. They have great names that are fun to say: *kata*, *wabi sabi*, *ikigai*, and *ganbette*. There aren't straightforward direct translation words in English to represent these concepts, so doing some research to learn more about them is advised.

With the popularity of Japanese martial arts, *kata* has become a very familiar word to most of us around the world.[15] We think of it as a set of steps in a defined sequence that we practice repeatedly to learn specific movements. The *sensei* or teacher will provide feedback while observing the intricacies of our movements. Over time the movements start to feel natural and flow. The *kata* may look like a perfectly rehearsed dance. *Kata* in essence is the cyclic learning by experiencing. (Think FREE method as a cycle.) *Kata* isn't about just knowing what to do, it's about learning through practice. We are using this word to mean a similar practice – in this case, we are practicing on improving ourselves. Failure is our teacher providing feedback on what doesn't work.

Wabi sabi is about appreciating and celebrating our imperfections.[16] Recently the art form *kintsugi* has become well known. In *kintsugi*, broken pottery is pieced back together to its original structure, but the cracks are filled with a gold lacquer. These pottery pieces are not just restored, they are now more beautiful because of their imperfections. Can we see ourselves in this light? Can we learn to celebrate how we are rather than how we think we should be? Can we see beauty and appreciate our own scars, failures, and inadequacies? *Wabi sabi* teaches us to see beauty in our imperfections.

Ganbette is the Japanese word for always moving forward.[17] In Japan, you might hear "*Ganbette!*" rather than "Good luck!" when someone is leaving and taking on a challenge. The western "Good luck!" wish implies that whatever happens is up to luck. In Japan, *ganbette* is a way of thinking, which focuses on looking internally for strength and resourcefulness. *Ganbette* encourages tenacity and resilience when facing challenges. The closest direct translation for *ganbette* is more like "do your best, don't give up, stand firm."

Ikigai is a Japanese word that means life's purpose.[18] It's the thing that gives life meaning and makes it worth living. We need to find this for ourselves, our *ikigai*.

Why introduce these Japanese concepts into a section on continuous improvement? In the spirit of continuous improvement, we've described life as a journey. Thinking of life as a journey allows us to reframe our thoughts about how we approach our lives. Life isn't just a goal or place to get to. Our lives can be about ongoing growth and development, enjoying and learning from all that comes along – our successes and failures. This leads us back to the final Japanese word from earlier, *ikigai*. Knowing our purpose or what makes us feel alive and fulfilled is what really makes life worth living. It will take a regular *kata* practice (*Focus*) of intentional reflection (*Reflect*) and ongoing practice (*Explore*) to grow (*Engage*). We will need to celebrate our flaws and imperfections as *wabi sabi* teaches us. Finally, we'll need to embrace *ganbette* each day in the face of life's challenges. This is a journey worth the effort so that we can celebrate our *ikigai*.

Creating a life-support network will build a growth-oriented environment

For our growth, learning, and development to be a natural biproduct of our failures we need to create a life-support system that will encourage our own growth-oriented thinking. Our support system might be structures, practices, and people that keep our attention on our higher purpose and help us identify interdependencies and synergies. We can strengthen this system by surrounding ourselves with other like-minded individuals.

By openly sharing our failures and successes and then celebrating when we, or those around us, take intentional, deliberate risks (experiment), we begin building a life-support network.

Each of us have some failure in our own lives that we'd rather *not* be open about. When we make it OK to share our failures and successes with those around us, we are setting the stage for others to contribute ideas and solutions to us, or we may be helping someone else feel less alone in their own struggles. Admitting our mistakes or failures is seen by some as a sign of weakness but by being willing to share our Faceplants we can help lift some of that stigma. The fact of the matter is that things are always going to go wrong in some way or another and mistakes are going to be made. Our strength is not in how perfect we are or how few mistakes we make but in how we deal with those inevitable failures. Hiding failure may be an option for some people but for most of us it's not the best option if we want to move forward without this heavy baggage. Ugh, we all understand how difficult this is.

Another way we can fortify our support network is by acknowledging and celebrating when we or those around us are taking risks, even small risks. Regardless of whether the risk is a success or failure, celebrate the act of taking a risk. We rarely take risks unless we feel the chance of success is very high or almost certain. Taking small risks can be a good beginning or a baby step to taking larger, well-calculated risks with higher rewards.

One way to expand our life-support network is to find an accountabilibuddy. Accountabilitibuddy is defined just like it sounds – a buddy to hold you accountable.[19] Don't keep a commitment to try something new only in your head. Talk to someone about it who will help you hold yourself accountable. This makes the thing you want to accomplish much more difficult to withdraw from.

Noël and Melisa are long-term accountabilibuddies, long before they ever heard this word. They have multiple check-ins and systems to create this accountability. They have a weekly shared report and a monthly, quarterly, and annual check-in. The quarterly check-in cadence is to examine the goals that were set. At the end of each 12 weeks, they reflect and check in with themselves. The practice has evolved over the years, but they keep up a cadence of accountability, which allows them to write and speak aloud their reflections. Their accountability isn't necessary to the outcome as much as it is to the reflection on their personal actions over the prior period. Noël and Melisa measure everything. They have identified Wildly Important Goals (WIGs) for themselves.[20] The time of reflection is not about evaluating one another's performance as much as it's about reflecting on what happened. Melisa and Noël look at what happened and try to understand why. They measure to understand their progress toward what they each say is important in their lives.

As a part of the regular reflection, it's important to discuss what we've learned with others. These lessons learned consist of reviewing what happened, writing about it, reflecting on and examining it, until we've come up with several things that we've learned from the failure. This is a great opportunity to share what's been learned with our network.

TL;DR

- Problem solving can be cool!
- Embracing our natural curiosity opens new possibilities for life.
- Limit the blast zone for failures with experimentation.
- Practice helps strengthen our learning muscles.
- Continuous improvement is a lifelong journey.
- Build a growth-oriented environment and network around yourself.

Where the rubber hits the road

In your journal, examine your relationship to your experimentation.

- Try being curious and truly interested in something that happened with someone important in your life. Then try questioning yourself. Ask open-ended questions of the other person and yourself. Think about several things that you could have done differently.
- Consider upcoming events in your next week. Examine several events in light of your expectations. What are small experiments that you might try to impact the outcome?

Part 3

Fostering others' FREEdom

Chapter 8

Sharing this work

When we first started this work, we were regularly surprised by the emotions that came spilling out surrounding our Faceplants, often decades after the event occurred. The initial phases, *Focus*, *Reflect*, and *Explore*, brought considerable clarity, an alternate perspective, and often a huge dose of self-compassion. And yet, despite gaining this new perspective, understanding our Usual Suspects and identifying our Tripping Hazards, we were still getting swept away by our Conspirators and still repeating the same patterns. It wasn't until we got to the engage phase that the switch finally flipped, and we were able to check our expectations *before* they tripped us up. By looking at the day(s) and week ahead and searching out Tripping Hazards, we were able to deflate our expectations to rational proportions, anticipate red flags, and not only interrupt our Conspirators, but channel our Liberators instead. This didn't mean we were able to avoid painful feelings, thoughts, and emotions associated with failures altogether, but it did afford us a sort of bubble wrap around our Faceplants that significantly reduced the blast zone and negative repercussions. It was as if the dial on our stress was suddenly turned down a couple notches ("Hey Siri, volume down 2!"[1]). The engage piece was the ah-ha! moment that so drastically changed everything. We wanted to share what we learned with everyone we knew as soon as possible, and so we did. We took our unsuspecting victims by the hand and dragged them down a rabbit hole of Conspirators, Tripping Hazards, Amplifiers, and Liberators to help free them from the same funk we had felt lift throughout

this process. This will be great! We will all live calmer, less
funk-filled lives – yay! Except that's not exactly how it played
out. We were often met with blank stares, confused expres-
sions, and awkward "can't wait until your book comes out so I
can learn more" deflections. It's hard to imagine that we could
completely Faceplant on the topic of Faceplants, but that's
exactly where we found ourselves. This reality was upsetting.
We knew this method was effective, and it was hard watching
people we care about fall victim to their own out-of-whack
expectations. We wanted to share this work, but how to do it
effectively required some experimentation of our own.

We've all had peak experiences or read about things that
we just can't wait to share with others. We want our family
and friends to do that seminar, read that book, go see that
movie, eat at that restaurant, or go on that vacation. We hope
that reading this book and working through failures from a
new paradigm has been one of those experiences. We hope
this book is liberating, providing more freedom around past
failures and creating the possibility of embracing future failures in a new way. We wrote this book so that we could share
our experiences with failure and give others some ways to
lessen failure's grip – shifting the traditional failure narrative
from one of shame and blame to one of learning and growing.
After all, how great would it be if everyone had more freedom around past failures, could anticipate default modes of
dealing with failures, and approached failures with a growth
mindset? Who wouldn't want that for the people in their lives?

If this rings true, here are some ideas we've come up
with for how to share this material with the people we care
about. The first and easiest way to share this work is to share
the book. While that may seem like a hopeless marketing
plug (if we're honest, it probably is a little), really it is one
of our love languages. The three of us regularly snap images
of the "amazing new book" we just got or share quotes from
books that completely take our breath away because of the
profound beauty and raw emotion they elicit. As a matter of

fact, we love sharing books so much that in addition to the endnotes that capture our references, we've also included a "Recommended Reading" section in Toolbox 4 at the end of this book. Books we want to read are in a queue longer than Santa's nice list that seemingly grows longer every day. But much like the saying "you can lead a horse to water, but you can't make them drink," you can give a person this book, but you can't make them read it, let alone do the work. Since sitting idly by and watching the people in our lives struggle isn't high on our list of entertaining activities, here are some practical ways to guide people in erecting their own failure scaffolding. Sharing isn't about force-feeding ideas to unsuspecting victims. Instead:

1. We can share from a place of vulnerability about our past failures and what we've learned about ourselves.
2. Share what's different for us now around the topic of failure.
3. Share how we have applied what we've learned in the book to our lives.
4. Share how we still get caught by failure's funk. No one is perfect; we will still have challenges dealing with failures.

We've invented and included some concepts in this book (e.g. Conspirators, Liberators, Usual Suspects, Tripping Hazards, Life Sentences) that are likely meaningless to those who've not read the book. We don't recommend sharing concepts that people haven't read about and don't have any connection to. That backfired on us for sure, and it's really no surprise. We found that we were able to more effectively support one another, friends and family, when we had the common language and book materials to reference. Unless someone has read *Faceplant*, talking about Conspirators and other concepts will likely just create confusion. We've all experienced a well-intentioned person enthusiastically wanting us to try something by using a lot of jargon to talk about it. It sounds like they are speaking a foreign language. We can't relate to what they are saying because we don't have the same frame of reference. Instead of pulling us in, the conversation makes us feel left out. Avoiding terms like Conspirators, Usual Suspects, Liberators, and Life Sentences can make the concepts more accessible. This book should not be used to "diagnose" others, and those terms won't mean anything to them anyway. We made most of them up!

With all of that said, there are tell-tale signs that someone is stuck in a reaction to failure, and we want to be able to support them in dealing with the reaction powerfully. An eminent or ongoing Faceplant in others is when the reaction the person is having to a failure seems like an overreaction; in other words, a disproportionate reaction to the situation at hand. Often there is a disconnect between what happened and what was expected to happen with a situation, and emotions have taken over.

Proclaiming to someone else that they are overreacting and need to just calm down adds fuel to the fire, often resulting in things blowing up in our faces. When we believe someone is having a disproportionate reaction to something that happened, we need to remember that we are judging their reaction based on the composite of *our* life experiences and expectations. Often when there is a disconnect in how we would handle a situation versus how someone else would handle the same situation, it is because we are making decisions and taking actions based on different pools of information. Forcing someone to "get onboard" with our solutions and assertions wrongfully assumes that our pool of information is correct and theirs is incorrect. Each pool is filled with different experiences that shape unique perspectives and absolutely feel correct to each person. To gauge the other person's reactions accurately, we need to understand the pool of information they are working with. Have you ever tried telling a teenager how you would solve a problem they are perfectly capable of solving for themselves? As a mom of four teens, Keeley knows firsthand, it doesn't end well. The main goal here is to get a clear picture of their expectations and the factors pumping up those expectations so we can better craft clarifying and grounding questions to help them work through their own options.

We don't need to be a counselor or operate outside of our capabilities to support others, but there are some ways we might be able to assist others when we see signs of overreaction.

First, encouraging a pause makes all the difference in preventing a spiral of emotions. The pause could be as simple as taking a deep breath, which stops the automatic response and

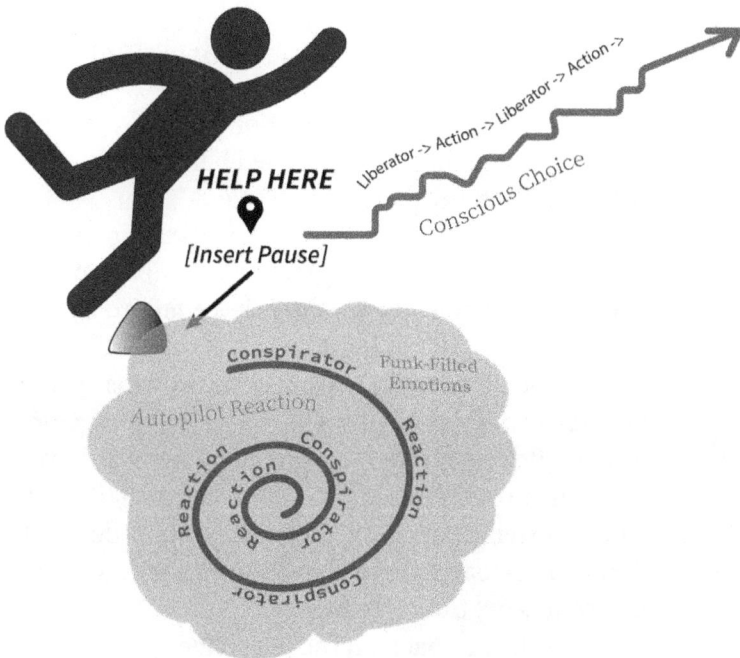

Figure 24   Supporting Others

allows us an opportunity to reset. Keeley's favorite approach to inserting a pause is through food and drink. "Wanna grab a coffee?" and "How about we get some lunch?" are two of her go-tos but even proposing a short walk can be a great way to introduce a pause. All three force us to slow down a little bit and breathe by changing the pace and the scenery of the day.

Inserting a pause creates the opportunity to ask clarifying and grounding questions. Asking questions with curiosity, no judgment, and no agenda validates the person's experience. Questions that we've found helpful:

- What happened?
- How are you feeling?
- What do you know to be true?
- What expectations did you have going into this situation?
- How are those expectations different from what happened?
- What would a realistic expectation be?
- Has something like this happened before?
- Do you notice any patterns?

Generous listening is one of the greatest contributions you can offer anyone. It helps loosen the grip of failure by providing the person we are talking to with the opportunity to see some things for themselves. We feel heard when people listen. Noël has a friend she talks with early Thursday mornings, and they offer each other the gift of being heard every time they speak to each other. Thursdays are usually great days! Through listening to each other, they often deal with emotions and over-reactions in their 30-minute call, allowing them both to start their day fresh.

When Keeley thinks back on the challenges she has tackled successfully, several factors come to mind. First, a mentor/coach/teacher pushed her outside of her comfort zone even though she felt unprepared. Second, she felt their belief in her – she could handle the difficult task(s) ahead. Third, they provided a safety net in the form of guidance, training, or simple words of encouragement when she would get stuck or felt like throwing in the towel.

One of the most important gifts we can give in this Faceplant process is the gift of belief in the person, especially when they don't believe in themselves. This doesn't look like cheerleading or being superficially positive, and it doesn't look the same to every person. Here's some suggestions for how to provide support and belief in others without superficial rah-rahs:

- Highlight examples of past struggles they have worked through, past successes they have had, past detours they have navigated.
- Help them identify what is within their control and what is outside of it.
- Acknowledge the difficulty of the situation and share past failures that you have experienced in a similar fashion.
- Help them to zoom out to five days, five months, and five years from now to see how the impact may change based on the measuring stick.
- Share quotes, memes, or videos that capture the emotional burden of the situation.
- Refer them to career counselors, therapists, support/interest groups, and friends who may also be able to provide guidance and support and/or help them out of their isolation.

One of the most important ways to support younger people, especially those in college or early in their career, is to provide them with opportunities to take risks while also providing coaching and mentorship to foster success. This will support them in building their confidence as they learn and allow them to expand their social capital – something that research has shown to be very important to young people.[2] Let them know they are capable, even when they make a mistake. Remember, unlike those with more experience, younger people are doing things for the first time. As a result, they have no frame of reference from their past as to whether something will work or not.

A conversation Noël frequently engages in with university students is to concentrate on what is within their control. For example, a student can develop a professional resume that speaks to their individual skills, experiences, and qualifications for a job they want. They can also meet the application deadlines, prepare for and arrive on time for the interview, and send the thank you note after the interview. They have no control over the skills, experience, or qualifications of other candidates who are also being considered for the job, the content of other candidates' resumes, or how other candidates prepare for the interview. Therefore, worrying about what the other candidates are doing makes no difference for their own job search. By looking at what they can control, students begin to experience a different path forward – from one of fear, worry, and deer in the headlights, to being empowered to take action regarding their job search.

The following true story is an example of how weaving grounding questions into a conversation helped insert a pause when Keeley's oldest daughter was experiencing a Conspirator hijack.

Keeley's story

When my oldest daughter, Maggie, went to college I went to therapy. I knew I needed to change my role in her life from protector (sometimes over-protector) to supporter and safety net. She did not make this transition easy. Right as Maggie was about to move into her dorm, she went through a tumultuous breakup with her long-term high school boyfriend, Tanner. For weeks it went back and forth, on again off again, each separation more volatile and devastating than the last, tearing holes in her heart, her psyche, and her sense of worth. I wanted to jump in, banish Tanner to another realm, and piece my perfectly imperfect beautiful child back together again.

Maggie was never one to share her inner world with me, so I was forever grateful that she did call me from school when things got bad. But I knew I had to tread lightly for fear of severing the flimsy thread of communication she had extended. This was the child whose motto since she could talk was "I do it myself."

If therapy taught me anything, it is that achieving our own ah-ha! moments through thoughtful questioning is far more powerful than someone spoon feeding you insights and "revelations" because that shit doesn't work. Truth be told, she didn't need me to "fix" anything, she *could* "do it herself," but knowing that didn't make it any easier to sit back and watch her struggle. Struggle with the loss of what was, struggle with the loss of what could have been, struggle to make it make sense, struggle to find her footing in this new unfamiliar world of college life and independence. Thankfully, shortly after Maggie started college, the ex-not-ex boyfriend Tanner moved to another state. Naively, I breathed a sigh of relief that this teeter totter from hell might be over. Much to my surprise, I got a call one afternoon declaring that she was going to go visit him the next weekend. (Curse you Expectation Disconnect!) Crap. I knew I couldn't tell her no, not just because she would have been more inspired to do it, but because she was now an adult and this was her decision to make, her path to forge. I also knew I couldn't say yes under the current circumstances. I needed her to be conscious of the danger and have an active plan to keep herself safe, so I asked her to go to dinner with me to discuss.

I started by reassuring her that this was her decision, not mine, and I merely wanted to understand her perspective better and make sure she was taking her own safety and well-being into account when planning her next moves. Maggie assured me she was and reiterated that she had already made the decision and would be traveling to see him out of state. Here's the 30,000-foot view so you get the gist of our conversation over dinner:

Me: It feels a little bit like a yo-yo, pulling your strings to keep you dangling. Are you adamant about going this weekend? Is there an option to delay and gather more evidence that this time it is sustainable?

Maggie: I really just need resolution. I'm sick of this going back and forth.

Me: OK, so you go there this weekend, what is your expectation for how things will play out?

Maggie: We'll have some tough conversations and figure out if we can make it work or not.

Me: Is there an option of doing that over the phone or coming to a common location that is familiar to you both?

Maggie: His job doesn't give enough time off to get back home, it needs to happen in person and can't wait, I'm going.

Me: OK, let's talk about worst-case scenarios just to prepare. I'm not saying this is going to happen, but I do want you to think about a plan for what you will do if it does. So, you get there, you have some hard conversations, and you decide this is it, we're done. Now what?

Maggie: I leave and come home.

Me: I get that, but how? You won't have a car if you fly there, you won't know anyone nearby, and you are not known for keeping your phone charged. What happens if this goes sideways, and tempers are flaring?

Maggie: His parents really like his neighbors, so I could go to them.

Me: That may be a good option if you can meet them early, but it seems like you have a little more planning to do in this area. I'm sure you can figure out a safe option, and I'm here to help if you need suggestions. OK, let's think about this on the flip side, everything goes great, you work it all out and yes, you are going to find a way to make this work long distance. What does "making it work long distance" mean to you?

Maggie: Finding times to visit each other regularly, talking daily.

Me: That sounds reasonable. Have you had a conversation about his expectations for how things will go when this works out? How does this impact your college experience? Are you still able to go out with friends or is that off limits? What are your expectations there? Understanding what both of you are expecting from this relationship and seeing if those expectations are compatible is going to be key to making it work.

Maggie: Yeah, we should definitely talk about that.

Me: I have one more question for you about your expectations moving forward. You have always been adventurous, charismatic, outgoing, and full of energy. It seems as if lately a portion of your spice for life has been dimmed. That is completely OK if you are choosing a new path that best aligns with who you are on the inside. It is not OK if you are trimming off pieces or toning them down to fit into someone else's idea of what they want their partner to be. You are glorious as a whole and will find someone who loves every calm and chaotic part of the brilliance that is all of you. So, when you look at this going forward, are there any pieces of you that you have to trim or dim to make this work or to fit into his expectations for what this relationship should be?

Maggie: I definitely stopped hanging out with my friends
as much – when I was with him before. I guess I have
a lot to think about.

Me: There is a lot to think about, and I am confident that
you will make the best decision you can with all the
information you have. I'm here if you want to talk
about it more.

When I dropped her back off at her dorm, I wasn't
sure what she was going to do. However, I felt significantly better knowing I had helped her to insert a pause
and think more clearly about her expectations for the
future based on the evidence she had from the past.
Maybe, just maybe, that pause was enough to interrupt
her Machine Conspirator who was acting out of the fear
of losing the familiar and determined to go visit regardless. (Spoiler Alert: She didn't go.)

When I finished writing the above story, I asked her
to read what I had written, see if I had captured it accurately enough, and determine whether I had permission
to include it in the book (I did). She found it
hilarious that her last serious relationship was captured
in a book called Faceplant and while it was definitely
a failure, she wanted to know how this was relevant.
I explained that my intent for the conversation was to
help her introduce a pause so that she could get out
of her charging ahead autopilot fear response (who we
call the Machine) and make a conscious choice about
what to do. I then asked for her impressions of that
conversation.

Maggie: I am definitely a Machine (laughing), and yeah,
it for sure made me pause. I remember that night
very clearly. I knew 100% that if you told me no, I

was going anyway. When you dropped me off at my dorm I had so many thoughts swirling that I went to the study room and made a list of pros and cons.

Me: That is a great strategy for flipping the switch to the conscious, so proud!

Maggie: I couldn't believe how the cons kept stacking up and most of the pros were from the early days of our relationship, not recent. At class with my college bestie the next day, I showed her the list and she was like "wow, uh, maybe you shouldn't go" and we both laughed. It's kind of embarrassing how stupid I was being about the whole thing looking back.

Me: It's not stupidity, it was your fear response trying to control an uncontrollable situation. The familiar (him) almost always feels safer than the unknown regardless of whether the familiar is safe or not. I'm really proud of you for sharing it with your college bestie, that took a lot of courage and is super helpful in bringing the truth out of the shadows.

And then as if to further prove the point that sharing this information is best done without the jargon, I went on to discuss the other Conspirators. I told her how I was often a Statue when situations concern me, but I am a Machine when it comes to situations regarding her and her sisters.

Maggie: (interrupting) What the hell are you talking about? (The force to be reckoned with was back, and my mama heart was full.)

Me: (facepalm and then laughing) Never mind, I'll be sure to get you a copy of the book if you have any desire to learn more.

TL;DR

- Don't try to explain any jargon to others.
- This book can support you and others in becoming aware of your automatic response (autopilot) to failure. An overreaction, or reaction that seems out of proportion to a situation, is a potential sign of an Expectation Disconnect.
- Asking yourself and others thoughtful questions can bring Tripping Hazards to light.
- Asking grounding questions can help focus attention on possible Expectation Disconnects.

Where the rubber hits the road

- Is there a relationship or topic that regularly devolves into an autopilot conspirator reaction (Machine, Magician, Statue, or Satellite)?
- What threat and/or Tripping Hazard is causing your reaction? What might the other person be experiencing in this situation?
- What additional questions could you ask to interrupt your Conspirator and clarify the "pool of information" they are working from to better understand their perspective?
- What Liberator would you like to unleash in your next interaction?

Conclusions

We've reached the end. A lot has been covered in this small book. Thanks for hanging in with us. It says a lot about your interest in and commitment to personal growth. Because we haven't provided enough opportunities for déjà vu (wink, wink), let's recap.

Although we have a new definition of failure and understand the value of failure in relation to how much we learn, that doesn't make the emotions associated with failure any easier to handle, at least not in all cases. Dealing with our own personal failures may still be hard. Fear of failure can still lead to avoiding failure. Blame, shame, guilt, and fear are still normal (though nauseating) emotional responses to failure. When our emotional responses are high, our brain can still get highjacked and the unconscious emotional response takes over, resulting in us responding in preprogrammed patterns. We know that it's impossible to learn and grow to our full capability when we live in fear of failure. Despite all these difficulties, failure and living our lives deliberately can get easier. Self-compassion is a great balm for failure. Practice and reflection are key skills to hone to make failure and growth less difficult.

Our brains are amazing! Two key areas to know about are the reactive part of the brain, the amygdala, and the processing or planning part of the brain, the prefrontal cortex. Our response to stimuli is in part governed by these parts. New neural circuits are formed in the brain when we learn something novel. The more we practice and reflect on our practice the thicker the myelin grows. Because our brains are not fixed at birth, we can continue to learn and grow. Learning requires four different activities: challenging experiences, practice, rich conversations, and reflection. Skill retention and learning result in myelin growth. Myelin, the insulation around nerve fibers that allows fast, efficient transmission of signals, grows thickest when we study, practice, and reflect.

Fear and avoidance are reasonable responses to failure, except when they are taken to extremes. Fearing failure is learned. The good news is that our fear can be reprogrammed. Rewiring our emotions takes practice. We can do this by interrupting our unconscious automatic responses and engaging our thinking brain. The struggle with the inner voice, primarily controlled by our autopilot, is real and can stop us. Remember our autopilot is responding to a perceived threat and trying to protect us. When the inner voice in our head is loud and strong, rather than listening to the story that can hijack us, challenge the inner voice to look at the understanding that is gained from our experiments. This subtle but important shift focuses our attention on learning rather than judging ourselves.

Our mindset is critical for learning from failure. Learning from reflection requires more than just looking back. Learning requires interrupting an Emotional Hijack and then taking the time to practice *hansei*. The FREE (*Focus, Reflect, Explore, Engage*) model, based on the practice of *hansei*, will allow us to learn from our failures. Repetition and reflection are key ingredients in building our failure immune system.

It's important that we experience and fully feel the failure and the losses associated with the failure. We may even need to wallow a bit with the disappointment and negative emotions, but only wallow for a short time. We don't want to allow ourselves to get stuck. To avoid getting stuck in this place, we need to limit the time we spend in the funk. Negative feelings can be catalysts that can help us more effectively process and analyze failure. Acknowledging the failure and our feelings about the failure is the first step of the FREE model. We want to get to the "what's so" regarding the failure. Whether speaking with another person or engaging in expressive writing, we can begin by sharing about our feelings as a way of appraising the situation. Failure can be a threat to our core identity, a threat to our safety, and/or a threat to our connectedness.

Authentic connection may require us to dismantle our old "infallible self-image." Writing opens doors to new ways of looking at our world. Sharing our stories gives us the opportunity to heal ourselves and others. We can't fix what we can't see. The *Focus* step allows us to sort what we know to be true from the other stuff.

In the *Reflect* phase, we take the time to examine our reaction or overreaction to a failure. We can learn to reflect and allow ourselves to see patterns in our responses to failure and ultimately work towards being the decision maker for determining our responses. The amygdala response is an Emotional Hijack from our unconscious, which brings out our Conspirators. The Machine Conspirator has us charge ahead at all costs. The Magician Conspirator will make excuses, justify, or sugarcoat events. The Statue Conspirator will be indecisive, hesitant, and just wait for it all to blow over. The Satellite Conspirator is the consummate follower and peacekeeper. Our Conspirator may be a pattern that shows up as our Usual Suspect. Expectations can be a Tripping Hazard when they differ greatly from reality. The gap between expectations and results is most tangible when we are rookies or late bloomers as adults. The unrealistic desire for perfection keeps us stuck with our Conspirators. Threats that initiate the Emotional Hijack can be amplified by comparison, isolation, and lifequakes.

Once we feel our appraisal of the situation is complete, it's time to transition from what happened to what's next. Understanding the true cause of a failure can be liberating. Bringing an open mind and strategic planning into our reflection, we can begin to explore what life has to offer. We can explore the many other response options available to us. Accepting that discomfort is a part of the failure and healing process helps us stand strong as we reset from Emotional Hijacks.

In the *Explore* phase, we solidify our new definition of failures as opportunities to learn and grow. Learning how to interrupt an emotional fire alarm is a first step toward freedom. We can learn to build in a breath, a space to pause, or create an emotional release trigger, when fear takes hold. Liberators are the conscious responses to our conspiratorial hijacks. Grounding expectations allows us to see clearly. Anticipated Events exercises and Pre-mortems can help us be better prepared to avoid Tripping Hazards, but unexpected situations will still happen and catch us off guard.

The final step in the FREE model is to *Engage*. Engage with life; after lifting some of failure's gravity from the past, we are free to create a new future that wasn't available when we were just reacting to failure in autopilot. By engaging in life with curiosity rather than judgment, we are living life with questions rather than pretending to know it all. We can find opportunities to learn and grow from our experiences whether they are failures or successes. The more we bring curiosity to our lives, which allows learning and growth, the thirstier we become to learn and grow more. Embracing our natural curiosity opens new possibilities for life. We can limit the blast zone for failures with small experiments. We can use problem solving as a means for structuring our experiments. Ongoing practice helps strengthen our failure and reflection muscles. The FREE model isn't a one-and-done experience – continuous improvement is a lifelong journey. Try not to do this alone – creating a life-support network will build a growth-oriented environment around you.

The FREE model presents an opportunity for growth though self-examination, which allows us to learn independently of the outcome. We've shared our failure stories not just as examples of how we did the work but as evidence that you are not alone on this journey. We can reset, learn, and grow allowing fresh starts and new chances for failure each day. On our journey towards freeing ourselves from failure's funk we have a renewed commitment to growth and moving forward. By regularly practicing the FREE method, we have the opportunity to change the course of our lives. With our newfound FREEdom from failure's funk, let's go forth and Faceplant.

Toolbox

Tool 1: The failure resume from Noël

Have you ever considered writing a failure resume? What is that even? Isn't a "failure resume" an oxymoron? Resumes are about making yourself look good, not showing off your failures. However, I figured writing about my failures on a resume could be a fun experiment that might put some puzzle pieces together for me regarding how I have dealt with past failures – and that is exactly what happened.

My approach to taking on this project was to be brutally honest with myself about my failures, have fun, and write like no one else would ever read this document. I hoped I would walk away from the experiment with many new insights about myself in relation to failure. I used the same resume template from my existing work resume, the one that makes me look amazing, and I used a similar format with a headline and an over-arching summary of high-level bullet points. My headline had to be catchy, poke fun at my flaws, and make me laugh. When I chose the experiences to write about, I included a combination of recent experiences and experiences from my childhood; some were more personal in nature and others related to work. My attention was on experiences that appeared to be the most life-altering, either because of how they made me feel about myself, what they cost me in terms of time, money, or health, or because I made a life-altering decision for myself because of the failure. I wrote the resume, then revisited it many times over the course of more than a year, each time getting more and more specific about the failures I included.

Writing the resume was powerful but reading it out loud to Melisa and Keeley took the experience to another level and brought out deep emotions. I saw repetitive patterns I hadn't seen in quite the same light before. My biggest failures revolve around not taking care of myself, mostly physically, but sometimes financially and emotionally too. I realized how exhausting these patterns are, how they have cost me joy and vitality, and in some cases have ended my ability to do things I really loved. That was painful to see. Through the very generous resume critique I received from my friend Jeff, I experienced how I still wanted to make myself look good in some ways. His questions and suggestions were helpful in having me refine my writing even more and get to the root of the failures.

When looking over the completed resume, I began to think about how these patterns developed and realized one main common denominator. Growing up as a child with a physical disability shaped a lot of my life. One of the hardest things for me has been the experience of some people doubting my abilities, and that started at a very young age. Being considered incapable by others made me want to prove that I was capable. That set me up to be in constant achievement mode (I'll show you) and play out the role of my go-to Conspirator – the Machine.

One example of my Machine Conspirator in action, included on the failure resume, was the El Tour de Tucson bike race that I wrote about in Chapter 4. While I don't want to take away from the accomplishment or the contributions I experienced from others that day, in hindsight it would have been better for me physically to stop riding and not complete the race. I didn't need to cross the finish line. My supporters would have been understanding, but my need to prove I was capable took over, and I didn't listen to my body. It was sobering to experience the huge loss that I had not ever acknowledged and most people in my life haven't even heard about until now. Talk about keeping secrets with our failures! I was so embarrassed and saddened by what I had done to myself that I pushed it to the background. Riding my bike was something I loved to do and something I miss.

As you can see, this resume had me see my patterns around failure that I didn't know existed. I highly encourage you to try this at home. However, beware, it's bound to bring stuff up – even if parts of it make you laugh. Treat it like an experiment, be brutally honest with yourself, write like no one else will ever see it, select those experiences that really have impacted you in life, and if possible, include one that has a success and a failure component, like my El Tour de Tucson experience. Finally, I do encourage you to share your failure resume (even if you don't want to) with someone who knows you well and loves you.

All the best, Noël

Noël Kreidler

South San Francisco Bay Area

SPECIALIZES IN CHALLENGES TO SAYING "NO," FEAR AROUND BEING SEEN AS INCAPABLE BY OTHERS, AND OF FAILURE

- Recognized perfection-seeker striving to avoid failure and be seen as competent and capable.
- Perpetually exhausted from lack of sleep and exercise. Work on projects late into the evening (*including this document you are now reading*).
- Consistently sacrifice health and well-being in the hope of being seen as capable by others.

SIGNIFICANT FAILURES

Kreidler Solutions | San Jose, CA (10/16 – 1/21)

Owner/Principal Consultant

Started my own business. It failed.

- Ignored need to develop strong and compelling value proposition.
- Overcommitted and managed time poorly.
- Avoided business development out of discomfort and fear.
- Spent most of savings before calling it quits and going back to work for someone else.

Marriage | Tucson, AZ (11/93 – 9/06)

Wife

Refused to acknowledge the truth of my failed marriage.

- Stayed married to a partner who I knew was not attracted to me and pretended that it wasn't true.
- Adjusted spending habits to accommodate partner's complaints, even though I was the main income earner.
- Beat myself up over accusations of things I did not say or do.
- Avoided getting help from family/friends in favor of maintaining the charade.

EL TOUR DE TUCSON | Tucson, AZ (11/05)

PERIMETER BIKE RACE PARTICIPANT

Prioritized completing bike race over my health.

- Ignored signs of severe hip and ankle pain through half of the race.
- Caused permanent injury to right ankle and was never able to ride long distances again.
- Kept injury a secret so I could bask in the glory of having completed the race and feed my "I'll show you" ego.

1ST ANNUAL TECH EXPO | Tucson, AZ (1/94 – 9/94)

CAREER SPECIALIST, CAREER SERVICES, THE UNIVERSITY OF ARIZONA

Hosted a technology showcase that failed on all fronts.

- Positioned employers and vendors on different floors making networking impossible.
- Failed to inspire my target audience, resulting in a 90% no show rate.
- Disappointed vendors who spent time and money to attend event.

ARCHMERE ACADEMY | Claymont, DE (9/83 –12/83)

HIGH SCHOOL JUNIOR

Earned a D in Advanced Placement (AP) Chemistry.

- Sacrificed confidence and my love of science by forcing myself through a class to prove to others that I could do it.
- Allowed this single experience to eliminate science as a future career option.

ST. NICHOLAS CHURCH | Newark, DE (4/78 – 7/80)

ACOLYTE (THINK *ALTAR-GIRL*)

Performed work I hated out of spite.

- Mom said I couldn't physically do this work. I said I could.
- Turns out I could, but I didn't like it.
- Kept doing it to prove mom wrong.

Tool 2: The Pre-mortem

The Pre-mortem helps us anticipate possible Faceplants and better equips us to deal with them when they appear. These are the steps to a Pre-mortem:

1. Brainstorm possible causes of the failure.
2. Identify the red flags that might lead to a failure.
3. Identify the mitigations that can be put in place to prevent those failures from happening and/or the actions to take if a red flag or failure appears.
4. Identify the timeframe when the mitigations must be put in place to ensure a successful outcome of the activity.

Let's look at an example. Say you're planning for the week ahead and know you have an important meeting with your boss and a couple of other executives to get some clarity on objectives for your team. For your Pre-mortem, you imagine a future where the meeting is over, and you are walking away more confused than when the meeting started. As you try to shake off the fog, you think back to what (could have) just happened:

Step 1: Brainstorm possible causes of the failure.

- *You had ten points and only addressed five of them.*
- *Someone went on a side tangent, and you ended up with four new tasks.*
- *Someone dominated the conversation and derailed the whole meeting.*
- *You went 25 minutes over the allotted time.*
- *Someone's phone kept pinging.*
- *One person was on their laptop the entire time (so much clicking).*

- *Two people kept whispering.*
- *Someone fell asleep.*

If you've ever been a part of a large meeting, you know that these scenarios are not only possible, but they can all happen in the same meeting! Ouch.

Step 2: Identify red flags that might lead to a failure.

- **You had ten points and only addressed five of them.**
  - *Red Flag: you are 15 minutes into an hour meeting and have only covered two items.*
- **Someone went on a side tangent, and you ended up with four new tasks.**
  - *Red Flag: Bob rolls into the meeting all fired up about a new conversation he had and the amazing opportunity it presents.*
- **One person was on their laptop the entire time (so much clicking).**
  - *Red Flag: three people walked in with laptops.*

You get the point.

Step 3: Identify actions that can prevent these failures from happening in the first place or mitigate them once they have happened. The following are mitigation actions and the failures they help to address:

- **You had ten points and only addressed five of them.**
  - *Red Flag: you are 15 minutes into an hour meeting and have only covered two items.*
    - ✓ *Create and distribute an agenda in advance of the meeting with times, responsible persons, and desired outcomes.*
    - ✓ *Appoint a timekeeper or set an incognito timer to silently indicate critical agenda time transitions.*

- *Someone went on a side tangent, and you ended up with four new tasks.*
  - ◻ *Red Flag: Bob is all fired up about a new conversation he had and the amazing opportunity it presents.*
  - ✓ *Review the agenda and meeting objectives at the start of the meeting.*
- *One person was on their laptop the entire time (so much clicking).*
  - ◻ *Red Flag: three people walked in with laptops.*
  - ✓ *Refer to the agenda for responsible persons' time slots and indicate the appropriate time(s) for them to access their computers.*
  - ✓ *Use a practiced script indicating that laptops won't be necessary for participation in the meeting so they can choose to return them to their offices or leave them closed on the table.*

So, now you've prepped in advance with as many mitigations as you can, but is that going to prevent these failures from happening? Maybe, but probably not entirely. Armed with the possible mitigation actions you created in Step 3, you're ready to move on to Step 4.

Step 4: Identify the best time to insert your mitigation strategy.

- *You had ten points and only addressed five of them.*
  - ◻ *Red Flag: you are 15 minutes into an hour meeting and have only covered two items.*
  - ✓ *Create and distribute an agenda in advance of the meeting with times, responsible persons, and desired outcomes.*
  - ✓ *Appoint a timekeeper or set an incognito timer to silently indicate critical agenda time transitions.*

⧖ *Redirect attention to agenda at allocated time slots.*

⧖ *Capture follow-up tasks for any item that is not complete in the designated time.*

- **Someone went on a side tangent, and you ended up with four new tasks.**
  - ◻ *Red Flag: Bob is all fired up about a new conversation he had and the amazing opportunity it presents.*
    - ✓ *Review the agenda and meeting objectives.*
      - ⧖ *Note the opportunity as a follow-up action and redirect back to the agenda at hand.*
      - ⧖ *Offer to schedule a follow-up meeting to discuss the new opportunity and how it should be prioritized.*

- **One person was on their laptop the entire time (so much clicking).**
  - ◻ *Red Flag: three people walked in with laptops.*
    - ✓ *Refer to the agenda for responsible persons' time slots and indicate the appropriate time(s) for them to access their computers.*
    - ✓ *Use a practice script indicating that laptops won't be necessary for participation in the meeting so they can choose to return them to their offices or leave them closed on the table.*
      - ⧖ *Re-enforce ground rules (channel your Machine Liberator!)*
      - ⧖ *Excuse people from the meeting if they have more pressing needs – with an assurance that outcomes from the meeting will be distributed.*

Finally, if you have examples of these types of failures in your past, you can reflect and ask yourself, "What Conspirator showed up in these situations?" Did you become a Statue when someone derailed the meeting? Did you become a

Satellite and allow the group to dictate the agenda diverting from the original plans and goals? By identifying a pattern or Usual Suspect, you can notice the repeating cycle of your reactions and consciously call upon a Liberator to help you avoid the predictable outcomes from your past. For example, if you were a Statue or a Satellite, you can leverage the Machine to redirect the group back to the agenda, refer to the ground rules if someone is engaging in distracting behaviors, and even practice scripts in advance to help interrupt the fear response. Remember, the purpose of the Pre-mortem is to help us anticipate possible Faceplants and be better equipped to deal with them when they appear.

Tool 3: Anticipated Events exercise

We all have expectations. It's part of being human. Our expectations can be grounded or unrealistic. Going on a first date and expecting "love at first sight" is likely an unrealistic expectation. As is playing the lottery and expecting to win. Unrealistic expectations are one of the most prominent Tripping Hazards we face. This means when we are faced with the disappointment of unmet expectations we might have an Emotional Hijack. At the very least, we are setting ourselves up for one. How can we be better prepared? You guessed it, by examining our expectations upfront and then looking closely at our reaction. Below is an example of an analysis by Noël. Visit our website at www.FaceplantBook.com for a blank worksheet.

Anticipated Events worksheet (example)

1. *Goal/situation/event: Describe the facts.*

   I have feedback to deliver during a 30-minute one-to-one meeting with my leader regarding the repeated poor timing of introducing new projects to the team and the level of frustration and disappointment it causes.

2. *What do you expect to happen? What thoughts are you having?*

   I expect I will be able to deliver the feedback, but the conversation could go sideways and feel like an attack. I need to make sure that doesn't happen. Depending on how the feedback is shared, it could be perceived that I'm not open to taking on new projects, which is not true.

3. *Describe what you want to have happen regarding this goal/ situation/event.*

> I wish to stay calm, clear, and respectful when I deliver the feedback. I want the feedback to be about the behavior, not the person. I want what I share to be heard. I want my leader to know that I appreciate the enthusiasm for trying new things, but I would prefer these opportunities to be introduced at a different time.

4. *What might trigger an Emotional Hijack, a Conspirator?*

> The question "How are you doing?" How I'm doing is irrelevant. I want to concentrate on the feedback I need to deliver. The Magician will show up if I get highjacked, and I will come across as whiny and bitchy.

5. *In the case of a trigger and Emotional Hijack, how will you handle it? Which Liberator could you leverage instead?*

> I will choose the Machine Liberator and direct the conversation in the way I want it to go. If I am asked, "How are you doing?" I will say, "I'd like to share some things that are on my mind."

6. *What would be a realistic expectation?*

> This leader is open to feedback and has been very receptive in the past. My worry that the conversation might not go well is probably in my head. I am usually good at delivering feedback because I get to the bottom of what's going on for me before I deliver feedback to someone else.

7. *What cautions, warning signs, or red flags might exist? What signs will indicate that a Conspirator is appearing?*

> I will start talking about how I feel instead of what happened. I could get louder and more emphatic when I talk. My leader might shut down if that happens, and there will be no dialogue.

8. *What preparation/mitigation actions might you take if your Conspirator appears?*

> I will stop myself, take a deep breath and say, "Let me get this conversation back on track."

9. *What was the outcome?*

> I showed up to the meeting, and the first question asked was, "How are you doing?" Since I had already identified that this question might hijack me, I executed my plan to shift the conversation. I said, "I am fine. However, I'd really like to spend this time talking about something that is on my mind." We agreed to shift gears, and I began to share about my current work and explained the negative impact on me and others when new projects are introduced at busy times of the year. Then, I offered timing suggestions that would work better. My leader was receptive, and we ended up having a great conversation where we both felt heard and understood.

10. *Perform a gap assessment. What were the differences between your original expectations and the outcome? Is there anything you would have done differently?*

> The conversation went better than I thought it would go. I was able to direct the conversation because I had given thought to what might hijack me and how I would handle it. My Liberator showed up, not my Conspirator.

Tool 4: Recommended reading

There are many books that we have read and referenced while writing *Faceplant*. There are so many that we loved and narrowing down this list of recommendations was difficult.

Rejection, failure, and fear

1. *The Gifts of Imperfection: Let Go of Who You Think You're Supposed to Be and Embrace Who You Are* by Brené Brown, PhD, is a great challenge to us all to live a life wholeheartedly.
2. *Right Kind of Wrong: The Science of Failing Well* by Amy Edmondson is a business book but at the top of our list of books on failure. Edmondson tackles the conflicting messages we get in industry about failure. These same messages apply in our personal lives as well.
3. *Black Box Thinking: Why Most People Never Learn from Their Mistakes – But Some Do* by Matthew Syed is a business book with great stories of how companies have failed and learned.
4. *Fear of Failure: How to Become an Action Taker, Stop Worrying, Overcome Procrastination and Perfectionism* by Wilda Hale.
5. *25 Ways to Overcome the Fear of Failure* by Kassandra Vaughn.

Writing and communication

1. *Exploratory Writing: Everyday Magic for Life and Work* by Alison Jones provides simple tools for exploring your inner thoughts.
2. *Supercommunicators: How to Unlock the Secret Language of Connection* by Charles Duhigg is all about how we communicate.
3. *Opening Up by Writing it Down: How Expressive Writing Improves Health and Eases Emotional Pain* by James W. Pennebaker, PhD and Joshua M. Smyth, PhD.

Curiosity and experimentation

1. *Both/And Thinking: Embracing Creative Tensions to Solve Your Toughest Problems* by Wendy K. Smith and Marianne W. Lewis.
2. *Range: Why Generalists Triumph in a Specialized World* by David Epstein.
3. *The Power of Flexing: How to Use Small Daily Experiments to Create Big Life-Changing Growth* by Susan J. Ashford is a business book with a great summary of research on personal and professional growth and development.
4. *Adapt: Why Success Always Starts with Failure* by Tim Harford.
5. *Problem Solving for New Engineers: What Every Engineering Manager Wants You to Know* by Melisa Buie is not just for engineers.

Continuous improvement

1. *Learning to Lead, Leading to Learn: Lessons from Toyota Leader Isao Yoshino on a Lifetime of Continuous Learning* by Katie Anderson may be one of the best examples of *hansei* in business.

2. *Ganbette! The Japanese Art of Always Moving Forward* by Albert Liebermann is a short read but Liebermann captures the "Do Your Best" spirit of the Japanese.

Mindset, learning, and brain science

1. *The Talent Code: Greatness Isn't Born. It's Grown* by Daniel Coyle.
2. *Emotional Agility: Get Unstuck, Embrace Change and Thrive in Work and Life* by Susan David, PhD.
3. *Late Bloomers: The Power of Patience in a World Obsessed with Early Achievement* by Rich Karlgaard is a great read for anyone who doesn't fit the early achievement formula.
4. *How We Learn: The Surprising Truth About When, Where, and Why It Happens* by Benedict Carey is a well-researched summary of methods of learning.
5. *Limitless Mind: Learn, Lead and Live Without Barriers* by Jo Boaler.
6. *Play: How it Shapes the Brain, Opens the Imagination, and Invigorates the Soul* by Stuart Brown, MD.
7. *Hidden Potential: The Science of Achieving Greater Things* by Adam Grant.

Inspirational

1. *Rejection Proof: How I Beat Fear and Became Invincible Though 100 Days of Rejection* by Jia Jiang is a wonderful story of the transformation of one man by taking on a 100-day rejection challenge.
2. *Very Good Lives: The Fringe Benefits of Failure and Importance of Imagination* by J. K. Rowling is a lecture that Rowling delivered to the graduating class at Harvard. There's good advice for all.

3. *Crash Test Girl: An Unlikely Experiment in Using the Scientific Method to Answer Life's Toughest Questions* by Kari Byron.
4. *Find a Way: The Inspiring Story of One Woman's Pursuit of a Lifelong Dream* by Diana Nyad.

Obstacles

1. *Effortless: Make It Easier to Do What Matters Most* by Greg McKeown.
2. *Struggle: The Surprising Truth, Beauty and Opportunity Hidden in Life's Sh*ttier Moments* by Grace Marshall.
3. *The Science of Stuck: Breaking Through Inertia to Find Your Path Forward* by Britt Frank.
4. *The Obstacle is the Way: The Timeless Art of Turning Trials into Triumph* by Ryan Holiday.

Notes

Introduction

[1] **Fear of failing:** "22 Fear of Failure Statistics to Change the Way You Think" Soocial (2025, blog). The article has embedded references to many other sources. While we've just highlighted a few statistics, there are so many more in the article. Available from: www.soocial.com/fear-of-failure-statistics/

[2] **Combination of humanness:** Amy Edmonson *The Right Kind of Wrong: The Science of Failing Well* (New York: Atria Books, an imprint of Simon & Schuster, 2023). Edmondson addresses why it is so difficult to fail well.

[3] **Oxford Dictionary:** Definitions from Oxford Languages. Available from: www.google.com/search?q=failure&sei=_N3dZ7ftGtOMwbkP3_rqiQs [Accessed: February 16, 2021].

[4] **Fear list:** Tim Ferriss Why you should define your fears instead of your goals | TED Talk (April 2017) and Susan Peppercorn *Ditch Your Inner Critic at Work: Evidence-Based Strategies to Thrive in Your Career* (Dover: Self-Published, 2017).

[5] **If fear is a particular concern:** Guy Winch "10 Signs That You Might Have Fear of Failure… and 2 ways to overcome it and succeed," in *Psychology Today*, June 18, 2013. Available from: www.psychologytoday.com/us/blog/the-squeaky-wheel/201306/10-signs-that-you-might-have-fear-of-failure?msockid=3e3a86fffa6f6fb13487970bfbc26eb0

The funk of failure

[1] **"Mistakes I've Made" folder:** Kathryn Schulz *Being Wrong: Adventures in the Margin of Error* (New York: Ecco, an imprint of HarperCollins, 2010).

[2] **"Even when we know that we were wrong…":** Kathryn Schulz *Being Wrong: Adventures in the Margin of Error* (New York: Ecco, an imprint of HarperCollins, 2010).

[3] **Blame:** Ben Dattner and Darren Dahl *The Blame Game: How the Hidden Rules of Credit and Blame Determine Our Success or Failure* (New York: Free Press, an imprint of Simon & Schuster, 2011).

[4] **Brené Brown** *I Thought It Was Just Me: (But it Isn't): Making the Journey from "What Will People Think?" to "I Am Enough"* (New York: Gotham, 2007).

[5] **Brené Brown** *I Thought It Was Just Me: (But it Isn't): Making the Journey from "What Will People Think?" to "I Am Enough"* (New York: Gotham, 2007).

[6] **Our brains are pre-programmed for regret:** Daniel Pink *The Power of Regret: How Looking Backward Moves Us Forward* (New York: Riverhead Books, an imprint of Penguin Group, 2022).

[7] **Ramesh Perera-Delcourt** "The Anxiety Equation in Cognitive Behavioural Therapy: A Simple Tool for Breaking Down Your Fears" in *Perera-Delcourt Psychology*, May 5, 2016. Available from: www.perera-delcourt.co.uk/single-post/2016/05/05/the-anxiety-equation-in-cognitive-behavioural-therapy-a-simple-tool-for-breaking-down-you. See also Aaron T. Beck, Gary Emery and Ruth L. Greenberg *Anxiety Disorders and Phobias: A Cognitive Perspective* (New York: Basic Books, 1985); Paul Martin Salkovskis, Hilary M.C. Warwick and Alicia Deale "Cognitive-Behavioral Treatment for Severe and Persistent Health Anxiety (Hypochondriasis)" in *Brief Treatment and Crisis Intervention*, vol. 3, 353–67, September 3, 2003.

[8] **Russ Harris** *The Happiness Trap (Second Edition): Stop Struggling, Start Living* (Boulder: Shambhala, 2022).

[9] **Home Alone:** John Hughes, writer. www.imdb.com/title/tt0099785/ (1990).

[10] **When dealing with failure, we've grouped fears...:** Dr. Karl Albrecht *Practical Intelligence: The Art and Science of Common Sense* (New York: John Wiley & Son, 2007). Thinker and author Karl Albrecht has defined our five core fears: extinction, mutilation, loss of autonomy, separation, and ego death. We don't want to dwell on these too much, just enough to share a bit to connect the dots between why our fear of failure can be so debilitating and why even the most harmless sounding situation might feel like a threat. Fear of extinction is really our fear of death and dying, which includes fears of flying, heights, etc. Fear of mutilation or body invasion has to do with our fear of feeling physically unsafe. The fear of mutilation includes things like spiders and snakes to infectious diseases like COVID to needles and dentists. The fear of loss of autonomy is our fear of being powerless, whether that's from confinement or paralysis,

aging, illness, or poverty. This fear might come from feeling confined by an intimate relationship, a work situation, or a parental relationship. Fear of separation is fearing any loss of connection, including abandonment and rejection. This fear might arise from relationships ending or deepening (becoming more vulnerable and intimate), an argument or disagreement, or from being ignored. Extended separation can also trigger this fear. The final of the fears is ego death. Ego death is humiliation or a shame trigger. Examples include fear of failure, criticism, bullying, public speaking, etc. More explanations can be found at Emma-Louise's Fierce Kindness Blog. Available from: https://fiercekindness.com/what-we-are-really-afraid-of-albrechts-5-types-of-fears/

[11] **The distinction between feelings, thoughts, and emotions:** Britt Frank *The Science of Stuck: Breaking Through Inertia to Find Your Path Forward* (Los Angeles: TarcherPerigee, an imprint of Penguin Group, 2022).

[12] **That create emotions:** Britt Frank *The Science of Stuck: Breaking Through Inertia to Find Your Path Fj2oorward* (Los Angeles: TarcherPerigee, an imprint of Penguin Group, 2022).

[13] **Narrative fallacy:** Ronald J. Allen "The Narrative Fallacy, the Relative Plausibility Theory, and a Theory of the Trial" in *International Commentary on Evidence*, vol. 3, no. 1 (2006). The concept was popularized by Nassim Nicholas Taleb. Nassim Taleb *The Black Swan: The Impact of the Highly Improbable* (New York: Random House, April 2007).

[14] **Especially for children:** Leigh W. Jerome, PhD "Generational Shame and Other Secrets Passed on by Your Parents" in *Psychology Today*, January 6, 2025. Available from: www.psychologytoday.com/us/blog/the-stories-we-tell/202501/generational-shame-and-other-secrets-passed-on-by-your-parents?msockid=3e3a86fffa6f6fb13487970bfbc26eb0. Claire McCarthy, MD "Think hard before shaming children" in *Harvard Health Publishing*, January 24, 2020. Available from: www.health.harvard.edu/blog/think-hard-before-shaming-children-2020012418692

[15] **Crucible moments:** Warren G. Bennis and Robert J. Thomas "Crucibles of Leadership" in *Harvard Business Review*, p. 2 (September 2002).

[16] **Failure in our lives:** Susan David, PhD *Emotional Agility: Get Unstuck, Embrace Change and Thrive in Work and Life* (New York: Avery, an imprint of Penguin Random House, 2016).

How we learn

[1] **Gary Larson.** Available from: https://screenrant.com/funniest-far-side-comics-about-cats-gary-larson/

[2] **The tortoise and the hare:** Jeremy Shapiro, PhD "Two Parts of the Brain Govern Much of Mental Life: Understanding the roles of the amygdala and the prefrontal cortex" in *Psychology Today*, November 5, 2021. Available from: www.psychologytoday.com/us/blog/thinking-in-black-white-and-gray/202111/two-parts-the-brain-govern-much-of-mental-life?msockid=3e3a86fffa6f6fb13487970bfbc26eb0

[3] **Unconscious or subconscious:** Michael Craig Miller, MD "Unconscious or Subconscious?" in *Harvard Health Publishing*, August 2, 2010. Available from: www.health.harvard.edu/blog/unconscious-or-subconscious-20100801255

[4] **Autopilot response:** Sylvain Landry, PhD *Bringing Scientific Thinking to Life: An Introduction to Toyota Kata for Next-Generation Business Leaders (and Those Who Would Like to Be)* (Montreal: JFD, 2022).

[5] **Amygdala hijack:** Daniel Golman *Emotional Intelligence: Why It Can Matter More than IQ* (New York: Bantam, an imprint of Random House, 2005).

[6] **Emotional hijack:** Daniel Golman *Emotional Intelligence: Why It Can Matter More than IQ* (New York: Bantam, an imprint of Random House, 2005).

[7] **Skill response:** Christopher Vaughan "Neural activity promotes brain plasticity through myelin growth, study finds" in *Stanford Medicine News Center*, April 10, 2014. Available from: https://med.stanford.edu/news/all-news/2014/04/neural-activity-promotes-brain-plasticity-through-myelin-growth-study-finds.html

[8] **Pope:** The full quote written by Alexander Pope is "To err is human; to forgive, divine." This quote can be found in An Essay on Criticism written in 1711.

[9] **Learning curve:** The learning curve that we are using is based on a 1979 model developed by psychologists Don Kelley and Daryl Connor, the Emotional Cycle of Change. The model has five distinct emotional phases of the change journey. Available from: www.strategies-for-managing-change.com/daryl-conner.html

[10] **Sometimes we need to stay in that place:** Daniel Coyle *The Talent Code: Greatness Isn't Born. It's Grown* (New York: Bantam Books, 2009); Benedict Carey *How We Learn: The Surprising Truth About When, Where, and Why It Happens* (New York: Random House, 2014); Adam Grant *Hidden Potential: The Science of Achieving Greater Things* (New York: Viking, 2023); Jo Boaler *Limitless Mind: Learn, Lead and Live Without Barriers* (San Francisco: HarperOne, an imprint of HarperCollins, 2019).

[11] **Closing doors and possibilities:** Wendy K. Smith and Marianne J. Lewis *Both/And Thinking: Embracing Creative Tensions to Solve Your Toughest Problems* (Boston: Harvard Business Review Press, 2022).

[12] **Experience complete overwhelm:** Susan David, PhD *Emotional Agility: Get Unstuck, Embrace Change, and Thrive in Work and Life* (New York: Avery, an imprint of Penguin Random House, 2016).

[13] **Primary paths to learning:** Daniel Coyle *The Talent Code: Greatness Isn't Born. It's Grown. Here's How* (New York: Bantam Books, 2009); Benedict Carey *How We Learn: The Surprising Truth About When, Where, and Why It Happens* (New York: Random House, 2014); Adam Grant *Hidden Potential: The Science of Achieving Greater Things* (New York: Viking, 2023); Jo Boaler *Limitless Mind: Learn, Lead and Live Without Barriers* (San Francisco: HarperOne, an imprint of HarperCollins, 2019).

[14] **Professional athletes:** Si Armstrong "The Importance of Reflection in Football" in *The Football Hub*, October 27, 2023. Available from: www.the-football-hub.org/post/the-importance-of-reflection-in-football

[15] **Game to film study:** Dave Spadaro "Inside the Game: How Players Do Film Study" in *Philadelphia Eagles* (website), January 28, 2018. Available from: www.philadelphiaeagles.com/news/inside-the-game-how-players-do-film-study-20309663

[16] **When we reflect on them:** Susan J. Ashford *The Power of Flexing: How to Use Small Daily Experiments to Create Big Life-Changing Growth* (New York: Harper Business, an imprint of HarperCollins, 2021).

[17] **Emotional memory, with repeated effort:** Britt Frank *The Science of Stuck: Breaking Through Inertia to Find Your Path Forward* (Los Angeles: TarcherPerigee, an imprint of Penguin Group, 2022); Lisa Feldman Barrett *Seven and a Half Lessons About the Brain* (New York: Mariner, 2020).

Flipping the script on failure

[1] **Carol S. Dweck, PhD** *Mindset: The New Psychology of Success: How We Can Learn to Fulfill Our Potential* (New York: Ballantine Books, 2007).

[2] **Often starts with reflection:** Serena Chen "Give Yourself a Break: The Power of Self-Compassion" in *Harvard Business Review*, September–October 2018. Available from: https://hbr.org/2018/09/give-yourself-a-break-the-power-of-self-compassion

[3] **Adopt a growth mindset:** Serena Chen "Give Yourself a Break: The Power of Self-Compassion" in *Harvard Business Review*, September–October

2018. Available from: https://hbr.org/2018/09/give-yourself-a-break-the-power-of-self-compassion

⁴ **Adopt a growth mindset:** Carol S. Dweck, PhD *Mindset: The New Psychology of Success: How We Can Learn to Fulfill Our Potential* (New York: Ballantine Books, 2007).

⁵ **Practice of *hansei*:** *Hansei* is associated with the philosophy of lean and the management practices of Toyota. A beautiful example of *hansei* in the life of a Toyota executive was written by Katie Anderson. Katie Anderson *Learning to Lead, Leading to Learn: Lessons from Toyota Leader Isao Yoshino on a Lifetime of Continuous Improvement* (San Francisco: Integrand Press, 2020). Another recommended read on *hansei* is by Mark Graban. Mark Graban *The Mistakes That Make Us: Cultivating a Culture of Learning and Innovation* (Dallas: Constancy, Inc., 2023).

Focus on the failure

¹ **In reflection:** Susan J. Ashford *The Power of Flexing: How to Use Small Daily Experiments to Create Big Life-Changing Growth* (New York: Harper Business, an imprint of HarperCollins, 2021).

² **Practice over reflection:** Susan J. Ashford *The Power of Flexing: How to Use Small Daily Experiments to Create Big Life-Changing Growth* (New York: Harper Business, an imprint of HarperCollins, 2021).

³ **Higher starting salaries:** D. Scott DeRue, Jennifer D. Nahrgang, John R. Hollenbeck and Kristina Workman "A Quasi-Experimental Study of After-Event Reviews and Leadership Development" in *Journal of Applied Psychology*, vol. 97, no. 5, p. 997 (2012).

⁴ **Sergent Joe Friday:** Jack Webb, creator of the TV series Dragnet, which aired from 1967 to 1970. www.imdb.com/title/tt0061248/

⁵ **Paul Tournier:** More information about Paul Tournier can be found on the website: https://paultournier.org/en/mdlp.html

⁶ **Brené Brown** *The Gifts of Imperfection: 10th Anniversary Edition* (Minnesota: Hazelden Publishing, 2022). Features a new foreword and brand-new tools.

⁷ **Thinking through my fingers:** Isaac Asimov. www.goodreads.com/quotes/452748-writing-to-me-is-simply-thinking-through-my-fingers [Accessed: March 23, 2025].

[8] **James W. Pennebaker and Joshua M. Smyth** *Opening Up by Writing It Down: How Expressive Writing Improves Health and Eases Emotional Pain, 3rd Edition* (New York, The Guilford Press, 2016).

[9] **Prompts for further exploration:** Alison Jones *Exploratory Writing: Everyday Magic for Life and Work* (Great Britian: Practical Inspiration Publishing, 2023); Bec Evans and Chris Smith *Written: How to Keep Writing and Build a Habit that Lasts* (Great Britian: Icon Books, 2023); Bill Burnett and Dave Evans *Designing Your Life: How to Build a Well-Lived Joyful Life* (New York: Alfred A. Knopf, 2016).

[10] **Deeper level of understanding:** The tool referenced is known as "5 Whys." There has been much written about this on the internet. A great starting place is the blog from the Lean Enterprise Institute. Art Smalley "5 Whys" in *Lean Enterprise Institute*. Available from: www.lean.org/lexicon-terms/5-whys/

[11] **About this experience:** Stacy Frazer "Navigating Emotions in Writing: How to Handle Personal Experiences and Emotional Wounds" in *Write It Scared* (Frazer's website). Available from: www.writeitscared.co/blog-3/navigating-emotions-in-writing-how-to-handle-personal-experiences-and-emotional-wounds

[12] **Four ways:** James W. Pennebaker and Joshua M. Smyth *Opening Up by Writing It Down: How Expressive Writing Improves Health and Eases Emotional Pain,* 3rd Edition (New York, The Guilford Press, 2016).

[13] It probably doesn't need to be said but choosing the right person to talk to about your failures is critical. Ensuring the listener is a safe person to speak with will make all the difference. A lot has been written about psychological safety in the workplace and there are a lot of parallels in life. A great place to start is with Amy Edmondson's work. Amy Edmondson *The Fearless Organization: Creating Psychological Safety in the Workplace for Learning, Innovation, and Growth* (New York: Wiley, 2019).

[14] **Helped, hugged, or heard:** Charles Duhigg *Supercommunicators: How to Unlock the Secret Language of Connection* (New York: Random House, 2024).

[15] **Minimize misconnection:** Charles Duhigg *Supercommunicators: How to Unlock the Secret Language of Connection* (New York: Random House, 2024).

[16] **Valuable reality check:** James W. Pennebaker and Joshua M. Smyth *Opening Up by Writing It Down: How Expressive Writing Improves Health and Eases Emotional Pain,* 3rd Edition (New York: The Guilford Press, 2016).

[17] **Tools and techniques that work best for you:** James W. Pennebaker and Joshua M. Smyth *Opening Up by Writing It Down: How Expressive Writing Improves Health and Eases Emotional Pain,* 3rd Edition (New York: The Guilford Press, 2016).

Reflect on your reaction

[1] **George Orwell** *Animal Farm* (Secker and Warburg, 1945).

[2] **I'm almost right:** Kathryn Schulz *Being Wrong: Adventures in the Margin of Error* (New York: Ecco, an imprint of HarperCollins, 2010).

[3] **Dunning-Kruger Effect:** Justin Kruger and David Dunning "Unskilled and unaware of it: how difficulties in recognizing one's own incompetence lead to inflated self-assessments" in *Journal of Personality and Social Psychology,* vol. 77, no. 6, p. 1121 (1999).

[4] **J. K. Rowling** *Harry Potter and the Sorcerer's Stone* (New York: Arthur A. Levine Books, 1998).

[5] **Nancy Berlinger** *After Harm: Medical Error and the Ethics of Forgiveness,* 1st Edition (Baltimore: Johns Hopkins University Press, 2005).

[6] **Stop paying attention:** Ayelet Fishbach *Get It Done: Surprising Lessons from the Science of Motivation* (New York: Little, Brown Spark, 2022).

[7] **Cole Porter.** Fifty Million Frenchman was an original musical comedy and Broadway production that opened November 27, 1929 and closed July 5, 1930. It was produced by E. Ray Goetz and directed by Edgar M. Woolley. Available from: www.sondheimguide.com/porter/fifty.html [Accessed: March 28, 2025].

[8] **Life Sentence:** Steven Zaffron and Dave Logan *The Three Laws of Performance: Rewriting the Future of Your Organization and Your Life* (San Francisco, an imprint of Wiley: Jossey-Bass, 2011). We are using the term "life sentence" slightly differently than Zaffron and Logan. *The Three Laws of Performance* emphasizes that we construct our life sentence during our childhood based on the experiences that make us think either "something is wrong here" or "something is wrong with me." In order to cover this apparent lack or inadequacy about ourselves, we decide to live our lives in a certain way; hence the term life sentence. We unconsciously choose our life sentence, which is designed to allow us to not only survive but also to be successful in life. However, it later becomes our armor that we cannot remove. As a result, our life sentence narrows our way of being and our views on life. Moreover, the authors

argue that life sentences become a mask that we wear that prevents us from having authentic relationships with ourselves and other people. Also refer to Bilge Azgın "A Review on 'The Three Laws of Performance' and Landmark Education" in *Journal of History Culture and Art Research,* vol. 7, no. 5, pp. 826–30 (2018). Available from: https://dx.doi.org/ 10.7596/taksad.v7i5.1786

[9] **Cognitive dissonance:** L. Festinger *A Theory of Cognitive Dissonance* (Stanford, CA: Stanford University Press, 1957); E. Harmon-Jones and J. Mills "An introduction to cognitive dissonance theory and an overview of current perspectives on the theory" in E. Harmon-Jones and J. Mills (eds.) *Cognitive dissonance: Progress on a pivotal theory in social psychology,* American Psychological Association, pp. 3–21 (1999).

[10] **The late bloomers:** Rich Karlguaard *Late Bloomers: The Power of Patience in a World Obsessed with Early Achievement* (New York: Currency, 2019).

Explore your options

[1] The origin of this quote is in question. Quote Investigator (online) has provided a thorough report investigating the source on February 18, 2018. Available from: https://quoteinvestigator.com/2018/02/18/response/ [Accessed: March 28, 2025].

[2] **Emotional Reset Button:** Dr. Karl Albrecht *Practical Intelligence: The Art and Science of Common Sense* (New York: Pfeiffer, 2007).

[3] **Baseline ground state as the afterburn:** Eric Berne *What Do You Say After You Say Hello?* (New York: Grove Press, 1977).

[4] **Alignment with your deepest values:** Susan David, PhD *Emotional Agility: Get Unstuck, Embrace Change, and Thrive in Work and Life* (New York: Avery, an imprint of Penguin Random House, 2016).

[5] **Add space into our pause:** Wendy K. Smith and Marianne J. Lewis *Both/And Thinking: Embracing Creative Tensions to Solve Your Toughest Problems* (Boston: Harvard Business Review Press, 2022).

[6] **Wendy K. Smith and Marianne J. Lewis** *Both/And Thinking: Embracing Creative Tensions to Solve Your Toughest Problems* (Boston: Harvard Business Review Press, 2022).

[7] **Contingency plans for those obstacles:** Susan J. Ashford *The Power of Flexing: How to Use Small Daily Experiments to Create Big Life-Changing Growth* (New York: Harper Business, an imprint of HarperCollins, 2021).

[8] **Increases the chances of success:** Gary Klein "Performing a Project Premortem" in *Harvard Business Review*, September 2007. Available from: https://hbr.org/2007/09/performing-a-project-premortem. See also Rebecca Zucker "Looking Back – and Ahead – to Set Your Team Up for Success" in *Harvard Business Review*, January 9, 2023. Available from: https://hbr.org/2023/01/looking-back-and-ahead-to-set-your-team-up-for-success

Engage in flipping the script

[1] **Proving and disproving myths:** Kari Byron *Crash Test Girl: An Unlikely Experiment in Using the Scientific Method to Answer Life's Toughest Questions* (New York: HarperOne, 2018).

[2] **PDCA:** Walter A. Shewhart was the first to develop a *repeating* cycle for improvement dubbed the Shewhart Cycle: Specify, Produce, and Inspect. Dr. Edward Deming expanded the Shewhart cycle into a four-step pattern: Design, Make, Sell, and Test. In 1951, the Japanese Union of Scientists and Engineers (JUSE) altered Deming's framework into the Plan, Do, Check, and Act (PDCA) cycle. Reference: "Plan, Do, Check, Act (PDCA) – A Resource Guide" in *Lean Enterprise Institute*. Available from: www.lean.org/lexicon-terms/pdca/ Eric Ries modified the model in his book *The Lean Startup* to Build, Measure, and Learn. Eric Ries *The Lean Startup: How Today's Entrepreneurs Use Continuous Innovation to Create Radically Successful Businesses* (New York: Crown Currency, an imprint of The Crown Publishing Group, 2011). See also Gemma Jones "The Experimenting Record" in *Spark Improvement*. Available from: www.sparkimprovement.co.uk/blog/the-experimenting-record Catherine McDonald teaches an alternative: Feel, Think, Learn, Act. See The Lean Solutions Podcast: "Rethinking Failure" Episode 2, Season 4 (January 4, 2025).

[3] **Why you were wrong:** Kari Byron *Crash Test Girl: An Unlikely Experiment in Using the Scientific Method to Answer Life's Toughest Questions* (New York: HarperOne, 2018).

[4] **Curious George:** H.A. Rey and Margret Rey *The Complete Adventures of Curious George: 75th Anniversary Edition* (New York: Clarion Books, 2016).

[5] **Problem solving:** Melisa Buie *Problem Solving for New Engineers: What Every Engineering Manager Wants You To Know* (New York: Productivity Press, an imprint of Taylor and Francis, 2017); Jamie Flinchbaugh *People Solve Problems: The Power of Every Person, Every Day, Every Problem* (Boston: Old Dutch Group, 2021); Gemma Jones "The Experimenting

Record (AKA The PDSA Cycle Record)" in *Spark Improvement*. Available from: www.sparkimprovement.co.uk/blog/the-experimenting-record

[6] **One step at a time:** Wendy K. Smith and Marianne J. Lewis *Both/And Thinking: Embracing Creative Tensions to Solve Your Toughest Problems* (Boston: Harvard Business Review Press, 2022).

[7] **Mental models:** The term mental models that shape our behavior was coined by Kenneith Craik in 1943. Recently, systems thinking and organizational learning has developed these concepts further. Donella H. Meadows *Thinking in Systems: A Primer* (Chelsea, Vermont: Chelsea Green Publishing, 2008); Peter M. Senge *The Fifth Discipline: The Art & Practice of The Learning Organization* (New York: Doubleday, 2006); Thomas S. Kuhn *The Structure of Scientific Revolutions: 50th Anniversary Edition* (Chicago: University of Chicago Press, 2012); Chris Agyris *Organization Traps: Leadership, Culture, Organizational Design* (Oxford: Oxford University Press, 2010).

[8] **Atomic Habits:** James Clear *Atomic Habits: An Easy & Proven Way to Build Good Habits & Break Bad Ones* (New York: Avery, an imprint of Penguin Publishing Group, 2018). BJ Fogg, PhD *Tiny Habits: The Small Changes that Change Everything* (New York: Harvest – an imprint of HarperCollins Publishers, 2020). Anne-Laure Le Cunff *Tiny Experiments: How to Live Freely in a Goal Obsessed World* (New York: Avery, 2025).

[9] **Putting bounds on our experiments:** Greg McKeown *Effortless: Make It Easier to Do What Matters Most* (New York: Crown Currency, an imprint of Penguin Random House US, 2021).

[10] **Wendy K. Smith and Marianne J. Lewis** *Both/And Thinking: Embracing Creative Tensions to Solve Your Toughest Problems* (Boston: Harvard Business Review Press, 2022).

[11] **How we learn:** Daniel Coyle *The Talent Code: Greatness Isn't Born. It's Grown* (New York: Bantam Books, 2009); Benedict Carey *How We Learn: The Surprising Truth About When, Where, and Why It Happens* (New York: Random House, 2014); Adam Grant *Hidden Potential: The Science of Achieving Greater Things* (New York: Viking, 2023); Jo Boaler *Limitless Mind: Learn, Lead and Live Without Barriers* (San Francisco: HarperOne, an imprint of HarperCollins, 2019).

[12] **Increased precision and understanding:** Daniel Coyle *The Talent Code: Greatness Isn't Born. It's Grown* (New York: Bantam Books, 2009).

[13] **Experts have:** Daniel Coyle *The Talent Code: Greatness Isn't Born. It's Grown* (New York: Bantam Books, 2009).

[14] Quote credited to Abraham Maslow, PhD. While there are many websites that credit this quote to Maslow, a biography and list of his publications can be found here: Abraham Maslow biography, quotes, theory and books – Toolshero. Available from: www.toolshero.com/toolsheroes/abraham-maslow/hero

[15] **Kata:** Gemma Jones "The 5 Steps of the Improvement Kata" in *Spark Improvement.* Available from: www.sparkimprovement.co.uk/blog/5-steps-improvement-kata Mike Rother *Toyota Kata: Managing People for Improvement, Adaptiveness and Superior Results* (New York: McGraw Hill, 2009); Mike Rother and Gerd Aulinger *Toyota Kata Culture: Building Organizational Capability and Mindset through Kata Coaching* (New York: McGraw Hill, 2022).

[16] **Wabi sabi:** Beth Kempton *Wabi Sabi: Japanese Wisdom for a Perfectly Imperfect Life* (New York: Harper, 2018); Nobuo Suzuki *Wabi Sabi: The Wisdom in Imperfection* (Tokyo: Tuttle Publishing, 2021).

[17] **Ganbette:** There are a number of books dedicated to these terms. One that we found helpful is Albert Liebermann *Ganbette!: The Japanese Art of Always Moving Forward* (Toyoko: Tuttle Publishing, 2021).

[18] **Ikigai:** Hector Garcia and Francesc Miralles *Ikigai: The Japanese Secret to a Long and Happy Life* (New York: Penguin Life, 2017).

[19] **In discussion** with Kari Granger. Available from: www.thegranger network.com

[20] **Wildly Important Goals:** Chris McChesney *The 4 Disciplines of Execution: Revised and Updated: Achieving Your Wildly Important Goals* (New York: Simon & Schuster, 2022).

Sharing this work

[1] **Siri** is a digital assistant from Apple. www.apple.com/siri/ [Accessed: March 28, 2025].

[2] **Important to young people:** David Yeager, PhD *10 to 25: The Science of Motivating Young People: A Groundbreaking Approach to Leading the Next Generation – And Making Your Own Life Easier* (New York: Avid Reader Press / Simon & Schuster, 2024).

In gratitude

The people in our lives make life worth living, and we're very appreciative to everyone for their support of us during the journey to write this book. At times, we have felt naked, vulnerable, and ashamed, even if you never knew we felt that way. Whether you knew it or not, you showed up for us in big and small ways. Even if it has been a while since we have connected, we have felt your presence and channeled special times we've shared.

Many thanks to all who've supported us throughout this book effort in different ways. To all those who completed the Failure Survey and to those who attended our workshops and trainings, we appreciate your feedback, comments, and engagement. To our beta readers – a gigantic Thank You! for all the feedback and encouragement: Janice, Len, Catherine, Jenny, Julie, Treena, Dani, Carolyn, Mary, Kalliyan, Aldo, Barb, Jeff, Jack, Renée, and Lisa.

Practical Inspiration Publishing has been a joy to work with – many thanks to Alison, Shell, Michelle, Lizzie, Nim, and Frances. Kenny and Enya for slogging through our VERY rough drafts and the invaluable feedback you provided. Our cover ideas were brought to life by Dick Skelt of Out of House Publishing Solutions Ltd and we couldn't be happier with the result.

Many, many thanks to Professor Wendy K. Smith for graciously reading a rough draft, seeing potential, and writing the foreword.

We'd also like to thank you, our readers. This work is our labor of love. Without you this project would have been for naught. We hope you can apply all, or parts, of this work in your lives and will share it with us and others.

A personal thank you from Noël

Jack, my partner in life! You are first in my life and the first for me to acknowledge. I am grateful for every day we have together because no amount of time will ever be enough. Thank you for being my biggest champion, appreciating me, and creating a calm place for me to land. I love the twinkle in your eye and the playfulness and adventure you have brought to my life. There is no way this book would have happened without your generosity, selflessness, love, and understanding.

Jeff, thank you for your friendship, compassion, and honesty. You have been a comforting constant in so many facets of my life – my brother from another mother. Your enthusiasm for this book has been very reassuring, and your thoughtful and compassionate critique of my failure resume had me release the remaining vestiges of needing to look good on paper.

To my parents (I have a lot of parents! – you know who you are), siblings, nephews and extended family as well as Jack's family (you are all family to me), thank you for always being there for me. Mom and Dad (wherever you are floating around), you did a good job! Thanks for understanding my need for independence and encouraging me to take risks. Every one of you are regularly in my thoughts, and though many of you live far away, I share stories about you all the time. Thank you always for your love and support.

Renée, Cindy, Maria, and Chris, thank you for loving and supporting me for many years. You have all been in my life for a long time and know me in multiple ways. You have also seen me fail and succeed. Even though we don't live near each other, it's like you're always near me.

Louise, you are an amazing listener. Thank you for making time for our Thursday morning calls. They always make a positive impact on my day. The work you do with people who are facing the end of their lives is extraordinary.

To the staff and faculty I work with or have worked with at Santa Clara University (SCU), especially in the Career Center and the Undergraduate Business Programs Office, I love working with you and am honored to be on your team, supporting students in realizing their career dreams. Thanks for rooting me on.

Finally, thank you to the students who work in the SCU Career Center, past and present, and students I have coached over the years, I am inspired by your willingness to try new things, fail, and learn. You bring great joy and laughter to my life, and it's truly a privilege to work with you. Many of you repeatedly asked for book updates, and your interest was pivotal to getting it completed. Thank you for allowing me to be part of your journey.

A personal thank you from Keeley

To my dad, who is the epitome of an uplifting coach both in sport and in life, thanks for always throwing your arm around my shoulder when I needed it most and doing your best to convince me it would all be ok, especially when I fought you on that idea the most.

To my mom, who always sang "everybody makes mistakes so why can't Keeley?", your annoyingly positive attitude toward Faceplants helped take the sting out of some of my worst ones and provided me with an ear worm that I have not escaped 40+ years later.

For my brothers, who have always had my back and who never let me live down my most embarrassing Faceplants, don't worry, I won't let you forget yours either.

Jasmine Matthews, thank you for helping me dig deeper with questions like "are you protecting the healing or protecting the trauma?" Your guidance and patience are priceless.

My New Smyrna Beaches – thanks for always being at the ready with a tissue, a belly laugh, a drink, or some strange combination of all the above. You make my Faceplants so much easier to take and life in general so much more fun.

Lisa Scott, the strongest and bravest person I know, and fellow lover of humans and science, I cannot thank you enough for being a safe place for our "baby's" first venture into the world. Your feedback was incredibly helpful and a big boost to my confidence that this baby was ready to take flight.

Maggie, Lindsey, Emmy, and Kasey, thank you for your continued patience as I endlessly stumble through this wild experiment called parenting, for keeping it real, and keeping me in check with your incredible clap backs, humor, and love. Thanks for also teaching me that the teenage eyeroll is a really good opportunity to check my own expectations because keeping 37 dirty dishes in your room is totally not a big deal, obviously.

I am still baffled that 22-year-old Keeley had the wherewithal to snag and keep such a fantastic human and amazing life partner. Thank you, Ethan, for catching me when I fall (which is a lot), keeping me laughing ("Did that just happen?"), and being the best hype-guy on the planet. You are my loudest advocate, strongest supporter, and most fearless wingman in all the crazy adventures we have embarked on through the years. I can't imagine ring-leading this circus with anyone else.

A personal thank you from Melisa

There are a few key people who were instrumental in teaching me to love experimentation:

- my parents, John and Mary Buie,
- my PhD advisor, Mary Brake, who encouraged me to get into the lab,
- my mentor and friend, in the lab and in life, Fred Khorasani,

- and my son who has helped me grow, learn and love more than I ever thought possible, Benjamin Alexander-Buie.

A thank you feels inadequate in expressing my gratitude. You all are my North Star, guiding my life's path.

Index

www.ingramcontent.com/pod-product-compliance
Lightning Source LLC
Chambersburg PA
CBHW031429270326
41930CB00007B/624